VOICES
from the
JAPANESE
WOMEN'S
MOVEMENT

D1318929

VOICES
from the
JAPANESE
WOMEN'S
MOVEMENT

Edited by AMPO-
Japan Asia Quarterly Review

Foreword by Charlotte Bunch

An East Gate Book

M.E. Sharpe
Armonk, New York
London, England

An East Gate Book

Copyright © 1996 by M. E. Sharpe, Inc.

Library of Congress Cataloging-in-Publication Data

Voices from the Japanese women's movement /
edited by AMPO, Japan Asia quarterly review.
p.   cm.—(Japan in the modern world)
"An East gate book."
Includes index.
ISBN 1-56324-725-9 (hardcover : alk. paper).—
ISBN 1-56324-726-7 (pbk. : alk. paper)
1. Feminism—Japan.
2. Women—Japan.
I. Ampo.
II. Series.
HQ1762.V65   1995
305.42′0952—dc20
95-43512
CIP
Printed in the United States of America

The paper used in this publication meets the minimum requirements of
American National Standard for Information Sciences—
Permanence of Paper for Printed Library Materials,
ANSI Z 39.48-1984.

| BM (c) | 10 | 9 | 8 | 7 | 6 | 5 | 4 | 3 | 2 | 1 |
| BM (p) | 10 | 9 | 8 | 7 | 6 | 5 | 4 | 3 | 2 | 1 |

Contents

About the Contributors

Abe Hiroko is a member of Mizura, a space for women in Yokohama.

Arimura Junko is the vice chairperson of the Seikatsu Club.

Ehara Yumiko is a leading Japanese feminist theoretician and teaches at Tokyo Metropolitan University.

Fukuma Yuko is a Kawasaki City public servant.

Hara Minako is a professional translator and has long been involved in lesbian issues.

Hayashi Yoko, a lawyer, has long worked on the issue of human rights.

Hikita Mitsuko, a farmer, is a member of a rural women's network in Okitama, in northeast Japan. She was formerly on the editorial staff of *AMPO*.

Inoue Reiko is the director of the Pacific Asia Resource Center, the organization which publishes *AMPO*.

Ishiwatari Sadako is a member of the women's section of the Miura Fishermen's Cooperative Association.

Kanai Yoshiko is the author of many books in Japanese, including *Moving Mountains: Women and Feminism in Japan,* which is scheduled to be published in English. She is a professor at Nagaoka Junior College.

Ann Kaneko is a freelance filmmaker and writer. She is currently producing a documentary on foreign workers in Japan.

Keira Tomoko is a member of Yay Yukar Park.

Kim Pu Ja is a member of the Uli-Yosong Network on Comfort Women, which was founded by resident Koreans to resolve the issue of the military sex slaves.

Kitazawa Yoko is co-president of the Asia Pacific Resource Center and an editorial board member of *AMPO*.

Kondo Keiko and **Makishita Noriko** are members of the Women's Space in Sapporo, Hokkaido.

Matsui Yayori is the director of the Asia Japan Women's Resource Center and the author of many books, including one work in English, *Women's Asia*.

Murata Noriko, a member of the Asian Women's Association, has worked to support victims of smuggling.

Nakajima Michiko, a lawyer, has long been involved in the issue of women's labor rights.

Nakano Mami is a lawyer who has long worked on the issue of women's labor rights.

Okura Yayoi is a member of the ODA Research and Study Group based in Bangkok.

Ooishi Yoshino is a freelance photographer.

Sakurai Yoko is a member of the Forum Yokohama.

Suzuki Mieko is a member of the International Movement Against All Forms of Discrimination and Racism (IMADR).

Takaguchi Atsuko is a member of the Apron workers' collective.

Takazato Suzuyo, an assembly member from Naha City, has long been active in the issues of women and U.S. military bases.

Tomizawa Yoshiko is a member of the Suginami Ward assembly in Tokyo.

Yamazaki Hiromi is a member of a group supporting the legal suits filed by former comfort women.

Yunomae Tomoko, a freelance writer, is a member of a group investigating the problem of spousal violence.

Foreword

Women often ask how they can be more global in their approaches to feminism. How can they know what is happening in women's movements elsewhere or what can they teach to make their courses more international in scope? This book helps to answer those questions. It is the kind of collection that I long for from every country in the world. It includes a wide array of diverse voices form a rural farmer to a lesbian translator, from lawyers to artists and trade unionists. And it spans the generations from veteran feminist pioneers to younger voices from the so-called "post-feminist" generation.

Too little is known about feminism in Japan in the rest of the world. Even today, I meet people who seem surprised that it even exists in a country so commonly identified with strong patriarchal traditions. Yet feminism in post-war Japan has a long and ardent history. I recall my own thrill in 1970 when I "discovered" a small feminists cell discussing women's liberation and planning a women's collective in Tokyo. For years after that I received numerous circulars from women's groups in Japan, and the English language newsletter *Asian Women's Liberation* published there in the late 1970s and early 1980s was my major source of feminist information on women in the region at one time. I was reminded of this history when over 5,000 Japanese women attended the NGO (non-governmental organizations) Forum held in conjunction with the Fourth World Conference on Women in Beijing, illustrating not only the country's growth in prosperity but also the continuing interest there in the question of women in society.

This collection introduces the reader to this history and to current debates among Japanese feminists. But it also offers fresh insights on questions being asked by women elsewhere. It explores issues that are very particular and yet universal. The authors are grounded in the specifics of the conditions and movements of women in Japan and in how Japanese policies affect women in other Asian countries. At the same time, these essays illustrate the pervasiveness of many themes common to women throughout the world—violence and sexual exploitation, the double day and the double standard, second-class political status and discriminatory working conditions—and yes, also delve into the divisions among women. It offers particularized perspectives rooted in the Japanese experience on many of the major debates of feminism in our day concerning issues like ecofeminism, racism, essentialism, prostitution and pornography, as well as problems like government cooptation and the troublesome relationship of women to nationalism.

A theme of great importance for feminists in the North explored here is how to deal with the impact of our nations' domination over women in the South, especially as the global economy dictates more and more of the terms of all our lives. Women in countries like the United States can learn much from these essays as we struggle to define women's global solidarity and responsibility for the policies of our governments and corporations in the world. One particular aspect of this for Japanese women that has gained world attention is the question of reparations for the exploitation and human rights abuse of "comfort women" during World War II. Several essays explore U.S. bases in Japan—an issue that recently surfaced with the rape of a school girl by U.S. servicemen in Okinawa.

These are only a few of the themes you will discover here. The best way to learn about feminism in another country is to go and live there. Since that is not possible for most of us, the next best is to find a good anthology that covers a wide array of views and helps us to see our commonalities and differences with women there. This is just such a book. I invite you to take a trip through its pages that will introduce you to women in Japan and return you to your own life and country with fresh insights.

Charlotte Bunch
New York, November 1995

Introduction: Looking Toward Beijing

Inoue Reiko

This book can be seen, in one sense, to be the third in a series of publications concerning the issues confronting Japanese women. The first was published in 1975, titled *Japanese Women Speak Out*. The second, a special issue of *AMPO*, appeared in 1986. And the third, whose articles make up the bulk of the present volume, was published as a special issue of *AMPO* in 1995. *AMPO*, an English-language quarterly magazine, has been produced since 1969 by the Pacific Asia Resource Center (PARC), a Tokyo-based citizens' group (or non-governmental organization). All three of these volumes can be seen as both reflections of the situation of women in Japan during the periods in which they were published, but simultaneously as demonstrating the more general situation of the women's movement internationally.

The purpose of AMPO has long been to act as a channel for Japanese people's voices, and to present alternative analyses of Japan and Asia. The foundation of the magazine in 1969 was part of the Japanese people's movement, and specifically at that time, part of the struggle against the Vietnam War. The focus of the magazine in its first decade was mostly the war, along with the rising opposition in Japan to megadevelopment projects and industrial pollution. Later its writers began to focus on the movements for democracy in Asian countries as represented, for example, by

Thailand, Philippines and South Korea. Naturally, the scope of this view also came to include Japan's presence in those countries. As we entered the 1980s, the view returned to an analysis of Japan itself.

In more recent years, PARC and *AMPO* have come to focus more attention on people's initiatives for alternatives and on global issues such as the international reform movement of the Bretton Woods institutions (the IMF and the World Bank, principally), and have become part of the Japanese coalition of NGOs working toward the Social Development Summit in Copenhagen and the United Nations Conference on Women in Beijing.

Women's Issues

When the first volume on women, *Japanese Women Speak Out*, was published in 1975, the main event on the international scene at that time was the United Nations Summit in Mexico City, and it is with the background of this gathering that this first tome was assembled. It was published just before the Mexico Conference. The international conference itself had a major impact on the Japanese women's movement in many different senses, but most importantly, it was practically the first encounter these women had had with women in the third world and was thus an exposure to the poverty in these countries, the necessity of women raising their voices for social change. It was also an initial exposure to the various dimensions of the women's lib movement in the United States, Europe, and the third world.

Japanese Women Speak Out reflects the women's lib movement at that time. The movement in Japan was very tight and consolidated, though its ideological influence came from a broad spectrum of women. At the same time, it was also a part of the social movements that were raising their voices to combat discrimination against the buraku, the handicapped, the Ainu, the Okinawans, and Korean and Chinese residents.

The second issue, from 1986, was titled *The Challenges Facing Japanese Women*. At this time, women were beginning to take on greater responsibilities in society, as can be seen for example by the leadership roles they played in the consumer and antinuclear power plant movements. The Equal Employment Opportunity Law was enacted during this period, and it thus marks a time of change for Japanese society more generally. In addition, it was during this time that women in minority groups, and for instance those in the movement against fingerprinting, began to see themselves and to speak out specifically as women. There was a rising consciousness among these women of the dual discrimination they faced even within their own communities.

Changes in Women's Position

The latest issue, upon which the present volume is based, can be seen to have a dual purpose. One purpose is to explore changes in the situation facing women in Japan, and the other is to form part of the preparations for the Beijing conference. It is thus both a tome of analysis and of action.

It is sometimes difficult to see this through the articles, but the past twenty years have in fact brought major changes both in Japanese society as a whole and in the Japanese women's movements, even while the very basic discrimination women face still remains harsh, as shown in the articles by Nakano Mami, Hayashi Yoko and the interview with Fukuma Yuko, which describe women's situation in the workplace and provide details of the legal aspects of problems facing women.

The 1993 *Human Development Report*, published by the United Nations Development Program, states, "The 1993 human development index puts Japan first. But when the HDI adjusted for gender disparity, Japan slips to number 17." We suspect, moreover, that the position of women in Japan may be even lower than this, considering the situation inside Japanese companies, in the academic world, and in politics, if we look for instance at the ratio of women among Diet members or local assembly members, or among the candidates for local parties.

We do find, however, that the situation is changing rapidly; for example, the loss of power and trust in the established political parties, including the Liberal Democrats, the newly formed Shinshinto, and the Social Democrats, as indicated by the results of local elections both in Tokyo and Osaka, where nonparty candidates defeated candidates with massive party support; on the other hand, the results also show at least the potential for a beginning for women's participation in politics, especially in local politics.

Japanese women are gaining power in our society, and we find today a bigger presence and influence from women in various social movements. On the other hand, the women's movement itself has become so diverse that no single women's movement or trend can truly be said to represent Japanese women.

Japanese women today face a great challenge: to take responsibility for creating an alternative Japanese society, and this is a task which cannot be separated from the realities of global society. As Kanai Yoshiko points out in her overview, the major issue confronting the Japanese feminist movement today is overcoming nationalistic feminism.

Looking Toward Beijing

Thus, this volume was partly intended as a contribution from Japanese women to the Beijing Women's Conference. As this book is being prepared, the women and movements that appear in its pages are busy preparing the Platform for Action for Beijing. In the years following the Nairobi Conference, the destinies of women have become every more intertwined in the global context, and women have thus increasingly taken on global issues. During the conferences on the environment and development in 1992, human rights in 1993, population in 1994, and social development in 1995, the voices of women and gender perspectives have become more and more integral parts of the whole process. Japanese women are gradually joining in these efforts.

Poverty will be the most important issue confronting the participants in Beijing. Many Japanese women will attend this conference, which is after all scheduled to be held in an Asian country, and they will come not only from Tokyo but from a multitude of localities throughout the country. Women's sections have been established in many local administrations since 1978, and this has helped to mobilize women on such global issues. For many, it will be a first challenge.

Japan as a country will have to confront two problematic aspects of itself during this conference. The first is equality, which, as in Nairobi, was taken up as one of the three themes, along with peace and development. Equality is still a goal in Japanese society, as can be seen by the still small participation of women in political and economic decision-making.

At the same time, Japan needs to take responsibility for the issue of poverty in the global context. This includes issues such as ODA, Structural Adjustment Program, and debt reduction, and how these relate to solutions to the problems of women's poverty. In particular, in the developing nations of Asia, many women are working under the exploitation of transnational companies, and to our regret, the Platform for Action for the Beijing conference is very weak in this regard. This is another great task facing Asian women, namely, the regulation of these companies in order to achieve similar working conditions in Japan and in other countries.

I

The Women's Movement

1

Issues for Japanese Feminism

Kanai Yoshiko

What did postwar Japan's "modernization" bring to women? What is it that they were emancipated from?

Women have been granted the ability to enjoy a certain freedom of diversity of lifestyles in modern Japanese society, which since its defeat in the war 50 years ago has come to be very proud of its economic power (though not its quality of life), and the situation of women in general seems to have improved.

On the other hand, however, oppression against women has become invisible and internalized, and the common identity shared by women has been destroyed. Japanese live today under harsh conditions; they find it difficult to share the difficulties and discrimination they face, and they cannot express the experiences of oppression as women with a common voice.

There are, at the very least, three possible types of women in present Japanese society, and the differences in consciousness and behavior among the three types go beyond mere generational differences.

The first is made up of those who lived under a predetermined "woman's fate." The second, their daughters, are those of us who made up the so-called"feminist generation." We were baptized by postwar democracy and by feminism, and we struggled for sexual equality and for women's self-reliance. We were forced to

etween work, on the one hand, and marriage and child-
the other. A third generation has now appeared in the
our daughters in the so-called "post-feminist generation."
Th.. do not hesitate to express antifeminist beliefs, saying, "we
are far from feminism." They dress themselves up to be pretty
and cute and fear the smelly and the dirty; it is therefore difficult
for them to share concerns based on the experience of oppression
of women, regarding the reality of an aging society, childbirth
and childrearing, or the environmental crisis.

This situation, in which the common ground of femininity is
collapsing, may go beyond the anticipated consequence of an
intensification of contradictions and inconsistencies among Japanese women. It may also create a deep crevice in the consciousness of women in the third world and in developed countries. In
today's world, where women are divided into two worlds separated by hierarchical differences in economic, historical and cultural conditions, women are inevitably situated in opposition to
each other, the freedom of women in the "North" standing on the
oppression of women in the "South." Japanese women, in particular, find themselves in a privileged position merely by the fact
of being Japanese. Unless we remain conscious of this privilege,
Japanese women will continue to stand on one side of a "vertical
domination" over women in the "South."

It is possible, moreover, that the movement and ideology of
feminism in postwar Japanese society may bear some responsibility for the situation in which the oppression of women has
become internalized and invisible and the common awareness of
"women" is not easily shared. I will argue that Japanese feminism in the years since World War II has not been able to discuss
these problematic areas.[1]

One End of Feminism

In the mid 1980s, the issue of women's self-reliance and emancipation began to emerge in feminist language. A debate on
"ecofeminism," which was triggered by Ivan Illich's "gender the-

ory," was the direct driving force for this discourse. Following this debate, radical feminists and Marxists launched into another debate on the issue of how to recognize the background of sexual oppression, or the question of "culturalism versus materialism." A third debate, over human rights theory, then erupted, pitting "human rights feminists" against "non-human rights feminists." These confrontations sometimes became so intense that they came to be regarded as virtual wars within the Japanese feminist movement, but each debate produced fruitful results, which raised the theoretical level of Japan's feminism.

The results of these debates are now being studied in a comprehensive way and are gradually being compiled into "feminist collections" or "anthologies."

The achievements of feminist theories in Europe and the U.S. since the 1970s have also, to some extent, been introduced and translated into Japanese. A survey of these works reveals that the theoretical level of Japan's feminism is at roughly the same level as its counterpart in the West.[2]

We cannot deny, however, that there are huge gaps between the theoretical level and the reality surrounding feminism and the situation of women in Japan. We must also acknowledge the existence of a gap between the theoretical level of feminism and the reality to which feminist discourse addresses itself. Furthermore, the so-called "backlash against feminism" has begun to gain some influence.

The harsh reality facing women today is demonstrated by the recent "job-hunt ice age" confronted by female college graduates, a situation which was brought about by companies' reducing their recruiting because of the continuing recession. In the face of this job scarcity, the powerlessness of the Equal Employment Opportunity Law (EEOL) and the shallowness of the "women's decade" of the 1980s were exposed. It would not have been surprising to see female students rioting, yet they did not even show any appetite for feminism.

Ironically, "post-feminist" slogans such as "no more feminism" or "feminism is dead" have attracted the interest of women. We need to keep in mind that the "backlash" phenomenon, in particular, has been strengthened by criticism coming from the younger generation, the "third generation" of feminists, rather than from outside. This third generation is made up of "daughters and sons" of those women who were baptized by the women's theory of Simone de Beauvoir and Betty Friedan and by feminist activism. They naturally accept the issue of women's self-reliance and gender equality. Because this third generation takes for granted the values and concepts their mothers' and grandmothers' generations struggled for, Japanese women face a difficult situation where they cannot discuss images of self-reliance and gender equality within a unified context, and they sometimes find themselves standing on opposite sides of the argument.

Some feminists say it is useless to argue against the post-feminist discourse of the third generation. Listening carefully to the voices of the younger generation, however, I think they are speaking not of "the end of feminism" but rather "one end of feminism," and that they are fighting to push feminist discourse to a new stage. It is journalism which twists their challenge to the discourse into a claim of the end of feminism. Unless we all become aware of this, these women will come to perceive feminism as having little to do with them, as being built on the resentment of a small and particular group of women. What women like me, who have been involved in feminism since the 1980s, need to do is to confront the real meaning of the third generation's challenge, which seeks "one end of feminism," and to begin the task of establishing a new theoretical framework for feminism that touches the reality of being a woman faced by the third generation.

With this background, I would like to begin discussing the characteristics and problems facing Japanese feminism. I also would like to raise some critical issues by analyzing the following points: (1) Why does Japanese feminism tend to be described as "housewife feminism"? (2) How should we classify the theoretical achievements and assumptions coming out of the debate regarding "ecofeminism" in the 1980s? (3) How have these issues been further developed in the various debates since the early

1990s? and (4) What issues are being raised by the third generation of feminists?

"Housewife Feminism" and "Feminism within Administration"

During the 1980s, the UN Decade for Women, as Japanese
women's organizations fought for domestic institutional reforms
in response to the Convention on the Elimination of All Forms of
Discrimination Against Women (CEDAW), and particularly during the heated debates on the establishment of the Equal Employment Opportunity Law (EEOL), female scholars, and in
particular those in the field of social policy, raised the following
critical question for feminism in Japan: Even given the energy of
debates on feminism and the huge introduction of foreign feminist
theories, was not Japanese feminism, after all, still a "feminism
for housewives"? This proved a crucial demonstration of the
weakness Japanese feminists had in understanding the situation
which "postwar patriarchy" was trying to maintain and rearrange.
The government planned to make a different use of social welfare and labor policies, namely to maintain postwar patriarchy.
For instance, the passage of the EEOL made way, on the one
hand, for dual lifestyles for women but, on the other hand, working women were classified into two categories: career women
and women who would be just ordinary assistants. It also paved
the way for the so-called "M-shape life cycle" (the "M" shows
employment for women over the life cycle, showing one peak in
the early 20s, followed by a valley as women quit to get married,
then by another peak in the 40s when women go out again to
look for work), in which women are burdened with both jobs and
housework. In addition, the government revised its tax and pension scheme in favor of housewives.

Japanese postwar patriarchy is a system suitable to state and
corporate society intervention into the lifestyles of both women
and men, turning men into "corporate warriors" and women into
"professional housewives" and a "reemployable labor force." In

other words, it is a "corporate-centered patriarchy, managed along the life cycle."[3]

Japanese patriarchy is made up of the following elements: (1) a system of controlling the family through lifetime employment, seniority-based salaries and enterprise unions (which also characterize Japanese management); (2) tax and pension systems which are based on the household unit; and (3) the Japanese welfare system, which is based on the premise of a division of labor and roles between sexes, based on sexism.

Why has the Japanese women's movement failed to loosen this patriarchy based on the control of life cycles? One reason can be found in the insufficient analysis and recognition given to "gender politics" by Japanese feminism. During the UN Decade for Women, a broad recognition emerged that the main cause of gender discrimination in Japanese society could be found in the sexual division of labor and roles, based on sexism, a reality epitomized by the "corporate warrior" and the "professional housewife."

To some extent, this sexist division of roles has loosened, but it cannot be said to have reached the level of "gender politics." At best, a model of gender coexistence has been introduced at the level of individual couples, in which men are encouraged to participate in housework and child-rearing. Transgender moves at the level of fashion have also become acceptable, as the mass media has started to show images of people whose sexual identities go beyond the existing divisions of male and female gender. Gender standards have loosened only at this level.

In feminism, gender is seen not only as a problem of sociocultural gaps between men and women. The main concerns on gender are: (1) that gender is a major factor in the prestige and distribution system in society; and (2) that social inequality emerges from this. What feminism struggles for, in one sense, is a reexamination of unequal power relations between the genders. This gender gap is a mechanism of sexual domination which gives a structural form to the inferiority of women compared to men, and in modern society the institutionalization of the "modern family" and the existence of the "housewife" bear a close relationship to this gap. The second wave of the feminist movement discovered that it was none other than the "modern family," which constituted the apparatus dominating women in modernity. The "modern family" seemed to ground gender hierarchy in a natural order between men and women, thus rendering its power relationship less visible. Consequently, patriarchal control in this private area emerged as something of deep significance for the feminist struggle. However, it is difficult to say that either this concept of gender raised by the second wave of feminism or the issues raised as "sexual politics," with their critical implications, have been recognized and taken root in Japanese society.

It has been difficult for "housewife feminism" to look critically at the housewives as a norm or at the social system which has institutionally supported this norm. As a result, feminist critiques of the sexist division of roles have not been able to confront the internal and subjective problems of sexual discrimination or to see the structural background of sexual discrimination as something shared by all women. A global perspective, which could lead us to recognize the complicated situation faced by women by looking at North-South issues, is also lacking. The limitations of this lack of a perspective of gender politics among "housewife feminists" can be seen most clearly in the field of sexuality, such as the issues of military sexual slavery and, more recently, prostitution.

These issues relate closely to the problem of wife beating in modern Japan. I would also like to confirm that the Japanese women's movement needs to go beyond "housewife feminism," which is being challenged by a new perspective which sees sexuality as a human right of women and sexual violence against women as a violation of human rights.

I would like to point out one more critical ongoing problem related to the above-mentioned characteristic of "housewife feminism," which I have labeled the "crisis of feminism within administration."[4] While women's participation in society is being promoted by various governmental administrative bodies, I fear that these moves might lead to the restructuring of the patriarchal system into a new form. This trend is being reinforced even while women are independently forming volunteer networks for the care of the elderly, or networks for the promotion of various "women's plans" in the form of women's councils. These movements, which are being promoted by administrative bodies, in the name of women's participation, may lead to the establishment of community systems of unpaid work by women, and are in reality nothing other than what Maria Mies has called the grand mobilization of nonwage labor by the capitalistic patriarchal nation-state.[5] The deep roots of patriarchy, which has directed nonwage female labor from the private sphere into the community, still survive in capitalism as a world system, and have been exported to the whole world including the South.

Thus, "housewife feminism" and "feminism within administration" can be seen as frameworks which reflect the critical relations between capitalism and women. Therefore Japanese feminism needs, urgently and inevitably, to take on the theoretical and practical task of going beyond these frameworks.

Ecology and Feminism

The year 1984 saw the eruption of a major debate on ecofeminism. The debate was sparked by ecofeminists using the "gender theory" of Ivan Illich. People argued over the question of whether to stress sexual differences or whether to consider these gaps very minor in the overall scheme of emancipating women. The debate finished unfruitfully, since the participants came to the peaceful conclusion that they shared the same goal.[6] What was recognized from the debate, though, was that there were reasons that ecofeminism was taken up by feminists in Japan at the time.

Motherhood and the fundamental value of women were taken up and praised against modern or industrialized society. Furthermore, there were frequent mentions of "Japanism," traditional values, and nostalgia for the ancient community. In short, we

were seeing a link between postmodern and premod
The thinking of Takamure Itsue, a prewar feminist, s
this kind of link can take a thinker. In the closed Japa
of the 1930s, she related her critique of modernism with support
for motherhood and the imperial system.

The ecofeminist movement of the 1980s emerged as Japan
was achieving solid economic growth and becoming known as
an economic superpower, as epitomized by the slogan, "Japan as
No. 1." People were beginning to question the American-Euro-
pean modernization model, and to talk of "Japanism," which
stressed tradition and national identity. It was quite natural for
other feminists to react to this ecofeminism, which emerged
from this situation. The debate was unsuccessful, though, and
this kind of thinking slowed the progress of ecofeminism in
Japan. In Europe and the United States, it was born as an anti-
capitalist, antimodernist, and antinationalist idea.[7] We have to
appreciate this difference.

We can see here the importance of linking feminist theory to
ecology, so that it can sharply criticize the present situation of ecology, where the elements of motherhood and eugenics coexist with
the work many women are doing in the anti-nuclear power, anti-nuclear weapons, safe food, and anti-global warming movements.

This phenomenon, quite particular to Japan, in which
postmodern theories are co-opted into premodern theories, is
happening not only to ecofeminism but also to Marxist feminism
and radical feminism. As I mentioned earlier regarding "housewife feminism," in the reception of "radical feminism" in Japan,
the dimension of gender politics was distorted and reduced in a
manner particular to the Japanese context. As for Marxist feminism, I should point out that Japanese Marxist feminism has yet
to adequately incorporate the level of awareness and argument of
recent thinking, which aims at theorizing the mutual relations and
contradictions between patriarchy and capitalism.[8] Japanese
Marxist feminism is still limited by the earlier discussions of the
1960s, which claimed that nonwage domestic labor was the material basis for women's oppression. We need to point out that

this discussion in Japan does not reflect the latest debates, which concern the connections and contradictions between patriarchy and capitalism.

It is also difficult to find views on women's status in relation to the state, capitalism and patriarchy under global capitalism, or any idea of developing this viewpoint into a theory of ecological feminism and the world system, as Claudia von Welhof, Maria Mies and Veronika Bennholdt-Thomsen did in their collaboration. The debate needs to go beyond the Japanese framework of "housewife feminism" and develop into a theory capable of analyzing the relations between women and capitalism and therefore explaining the globalization of capitalism and the influx of immigrant workers.

The Lack of Radical Feminism

Until now, patriarchy has been understood as the domination of women by men and of young men by their elders. With the second wave of feminism, this concept was "rediscovered" as a key concept problematizing the cultural, psychological and material basis for the oppression of women, rooted in modern systems linked to the formation of modern private realms such as sexuality and the family. Feminism came to the concept of patriarchy in the context of modern society by denying the analysis which reduced the basis of oppression simply to modernization or class contradictions. It was only with this concept of patriarchy that they could find a basis to criticize the oppression of women living in unequal, gender-based orders or power relationships in modern society. So the second wave of feminism was deeply tied to the idea of patriarchy.

In Japan, however, the image of patriarchy is different. Until War World II, everything in our society was tied to the family system, the "*ie*," so the word "patriarchy" immediately reminds people of the prewar, premodern oppression. Thus it tends to be difficult to see that "patriarchy" was originally a concept introduced into feminism in order to problematize the psychological and material background of women's oppression, which has its particular basis in modern society.

In Marxist feminism, which accepted a theory of radical feminism which defined patriarchy as different from capitalism in terms of its oppression of women, the concept of patriarchy was developed as material background for oppression. Marxist feminists developed the concepts of domestic and reproductive labor and contributed to an analysis of capitalism as a system to create nonwage domestic labor. Moreover, they continue to analyze and theorize the system which makes women engage in nonwage domestic labor, and to connect this analysis to a viewpoint which analyzes the relation between capital accumulation and women's labor. They have also begun to theorize the feminization of labor, which, with economic globalization, has begun to affect women in developing countries.

By analyzing the recognition Japanese feminism has given to the oppression of women theorized by radical and Marxist feminists, we can see the issues that have been ignored in feminist theory and movement here, and the reasons why they have been ignored. Here I stress that radical feminism has not taken root in Japan. We have not made sufficient efforts to analyze the cultural and psychological oppression of women, which could be explained by linking the concepts of patriarchy and gender. The concept of gender has gained broad recognition in Japanese feminism, while patriarchy has faced strong resistance. The concept of gender, however, was developed mainly in sociology. This means that Japanese feminists have ignored the issues of gender politics and power relations between women and men, which have been the foci of radical feminists. This is the reason, I suppose, why Ehara Yumiko called for a revival of radical feminism in the feminist scene following the debates in the 1980s.[9]

Shiota Sakiko, for her part, called Japanese feminism in the 1980s "housewife feminism."[10] This was an important critique of how feminism and the women's movement failed to react to reactionary tendencies such as the revision of taxation and welfare laws to promote a further division of labor, in spite of the fact that the division of labor had been under constant criticism during the UN Decade for Women. Ehara is promoting radical feminism for precisely the same reason. If we look at such phenomena as domestic violence, the large number of abortions, substantive divorces (where the wife and husband live in the same house but no longer even speak to each other), we can see that Japanese women are suffering, despite the image of happiness and freedom given to them. Consciousness concerning women's rights such as independence and self-determination has not taken root in Japan. This fact is related to the theoretical issue of feminism and the development of women's lib in Japan. "Freedom of choice" with regard to abortion is another element that has worked to make the feminism movement in Japan as it is.

Escaping from "Housewife Feminism"

I would now like to sum up the three major issues dealt with by the second wave of feminism: (1) equality in employment and the sexual division of labor; (2) domestic labor and reproduction; and (3) an overall demand for sexual independence and self-determination, developing out of the concrete issue of the demand for freedom of abortion.

Many efforts, both globally and domestically, have been made on behalf of these issues since the UN Decade for Women, particularly from Marxist and radical feminists.

In Japan, though, "housewife feminism" has influenced every movement, and the real demands made by women were distorted. In regard to the first issue—creating equality in work opportunities and abolishing the sexual division of labor—women failed to escape from their positions as housewives and merely tried to get their husbands involved in housework and child-care. These efforts were not able to come close to achieving radical changes in society, such as the establishment of equal labor rights for women and men, or of a social system where women and men could work and live together.

The second issue, the reevaluation of domestic labor and re-productive rights, has led to an expansion of the rights or space held by women as housewives, but has led neither to gaining the right of independence as individuals nor to the formulation of political demands for social change by raising awareness about reproductive rights in society. The feminist movement has the task of making political proposals in the field of reproductive rights because the rights of women which were protected by Japanese patriarchy are now being threatened along with the collapse of the family system inherent in the so-called "1955 system" (the conservative-progressive political division), in which women were protected as family members by the government's welfare system and by the wage systems of private companies. It is now time for the women's movements to escape from "house-wife feminism."

On the third issue, the discussion on sexual self-determination with the freedom of abortion, the least progress has been made. The debate on the issue of abortion has been different in Japan than in Europe, where this issue held the importance for the second wave that the issue of women's suffrage had for the first.

Abortion became partially legalized after World War II as a means of population control. Women were given the right to have abortions for economic as well as eugenic reasons. As a result, the freedom of abortion and access to the pill did not become political issues in the feminist movement. They emerged as an issue only when there was a proposal to amend the Eugenics Protection Act to remove the economic reasons clause. This would have made it substantially more difficult for women to have abortions, so the focus became not the question of abortion but rather the question of banning abortions. This movement has been successful, however, since the focus on the correctness of the ban has allowed many women from different positions on abortion to join in. The movement included both conservative women, who accepted the dominant theory or who preferred to preserve the status quo, and radical women, who opposed eugenics theory. Though there were major theoretical contradictions, the discussion did not lead to political debate but rather brought success to the movement.

This evaluation was made by Iwamoto Misako, a feminist. She has also reflected that Japanese women lacked the subjectivity to ask for reproductive rights and self-determination in the 1980s, and that in the 1990s Japanese women have finally reached the starting point from which to look for a new subjective identity for reproductive rights.[11]

Feminism in the 1990s

Following the era of ecofeminism, there were debates on whether women should take their children to their workplaces. This was dubbed the "Agnes phenomenon," after a famous singer who sparked discussion within the entertainment community, journalism, as well as feminism, by always bringing her baby to her concerts and recording sessions.[12]

This debate was quite natural given the rapidity of the feminization of labor. Many other debates have emerged from this. One feminist began to insist that all women withdraw from the labor market,[13] and ecofeminists began to discuss how to feminize men instead of unfeminizing women as a way to reduce the gaps. In short, this debate went in the direction of reproductive rights.

Next, I would like to discuss two points which deviate from the previous discussion, but which illustrate the debates occurring in the feminist movement after ecofeminism. One is the debate between materialists and culturalists, and the other between advocates of human rights feminism and other feminists.[14]

The debate between materialists and culturalists mirrors that between Marxist and radical feminists. It reflects the problem of the reception of Marxist feminism in Japan, as discussed above. According to the culturalists, the Marxist theoretical paradigm, which reduces everything to economics, and which therefore considers nonwage domestic labor as both the material basis for women's oppression and the basis for the formation of women as a class, cannot fully grasp modern patriarchy, which creates the modern family system and the modern housewife. This is why culturalists who advocate analyzing oppression with regard to the formation of women's subjectivities stress making feminist theory more precise as a social theory, through a "revival" of radical feminism and through the use of ethnomethodological arguments, deriving in part from Foucault's theory of power. They aim to create a social theory which can explain in detail the structures of invisible power functions; how oppression is structured in language and in discourse; how women's subjectivities are formed within the male-centered linguistic order; how women internalize oppression through this very process of the formation of their subjectivities; and how women then choose to become involved in subordinate relations through "unwilling choices."

I would like to point out that most progressive theories for eliminating discrimination against women in Japan have been formulated by people with this viewpoint. Even though few people are interested in post-Marxist feminist theories by European Gramscian feminists like Ernesto Laclau and Chantal Mouffe, we can expect more fruitful results if moves to create new feminist theories respond to their understanding of materialism beyond political and economic systems, as well as their critical views. Some of their works are now being translated.[15]

The reason this debate took the form of materialists versus culturalists is that a group which called itself the "cultural deconstructive feminists" entered the debate and launched an argument opposing the Marxist feminists' cognitive framework of women's oppression. They insisted that sexual discrimination was rooted in Buddhism and in ancient Japanese traditions such as the politics of harmony (*wa*) and the theory of place (*ba*). They traced it back to the era of Shotoku Taishi (ca. A.D. 6–7) rather than to Confucianism, which is a conventional view. The roots of the discrimination, they said, remain in sexism in present culture. This can be seen, they said, in issues such as military-forced prostitution and those surrounding sexuality, such as prostitution and pornographic culture.[16]

The second debate, which concerned human rights feminism and non-human rights feminism, was in fact quite similar to the debate between the materialists and the culturalists. The focus, though, was on whether it was better to stress the concept of women or of human rights. Was it better to push for minority rights for women or for human rights as a common concept that went beyond the position of women? In other words, it concerned whether feminism should question only the problems of women or whether it should question the entire system of discrimination and oppression which exists in social and cultural structures.[17]

This debate has not yet been settled and has spread in scope to a debate over the goal of feminism: metaphorically speaking, should we be eating steaks in polluted cities or rice-balls under a blue sky? What should be our image of the emancipation of women?[18]

Another important debate concerns women and the military. Women's demands for equal opportunity to join the military have culminated in demands for equal rights for women to engage in military combat.[19] Can we take this simply as an expansion of the freedom of occupation or of women's self-determination? And what about the rights of women working in the sex industry? Should their right to self-determination be accepted unconditionally? Do women have the right to sell sex or their bodies? If we allow for the freedom of choice in selling one's body or sex, feminism must give up its opposition to prostitution. Recently, the mass media has featured examples of high school students becoming involved in the commodification of sexuality in, for instance, telephone clubs or stores where girls sell their used school uniforms or underwear to men. How should feminism look at this? The principle of harm to others which forms the traditional basis of liberalism and freedom of speech cannot deal with this question of self-determination. Present theories of feminism which depend on ideas of "equality" and "fundamental rights" cannot deal fully with the new ideas of self-determination and sexual independence, according to which prostitution cannot be called wrong and the commodification of sexuality cannot be criticized. Feminists today face these difficult questions.

Current Issues for the Japanese Feminist Movement

The first issue that the feminist movement faces today is the overcoming of nationalistic feminism. One positive element in this struggle is the emergence of a feminist movement by resident Koreans in Japan. The movement here is being challenged by these women on the issues of "comfort women" and the question of the identity of the resident Koreans. They question the relationships between feminism and nationalism and between feminism and the power structure.

A related issue is how we can conceive of the universality of "women's oppression," given the enormous economic gaps and the different backgrounds of women of the South and the North. The presence of resident Koreans and other Asians as "significant others" forms an objective mirror to correct the distortions of our ethnocentric Japanese feminism. A second issue is the formation of theories and movements of ecological feminism. We must consider the destruction of people's lives and of nature (including the nature and environment inside our bodies) that has gone on in the background of our rich life and unlimited commercialization and consumerism. In relation to Asian and third world countries, we cannot avoid responsibility for the crimes we have committed by destroying nature and creating poverty. This consideration is important in preventing ecological feminism from contributing to reactionary ideologies that celebrate motherhood in premodern communities, or to nationalist ideologies such as Japanism. The first issue I described above becomes even more significant as a perspective that should help ecological feminism in overcoming such self-centered pleasure-seeking ideologies.

A third issue is the need to create theories to propose alternatives to networking-patriarchy or network-managed societies. As I mentioned before, in Japanese society, where there is no independent subjective force capable of being an alternative to the corporate society or to the strong nation-state, there is a strong possibility that "feminism within administration" might be used as the theoretical basis for a large-scale reorganization and exploitation of female nonwage labor.

Especially as people look for a new style of production and a well-equipped public welfare system to cope with an aging society with few children, there is a need for common cooperative and collective spaces composed of many independent individuals and a public space created by a diversity of citizens. These spaces should be developed as an independent third sector of citizens, to form an alternative to the sectors of government and business. We must create self-determination in our lifestyles, and break free of company-centered patriarchy. As a precondition to this, we should redefine the meaning of self-determination for women and minorities. This is why I stress the revival of radical feminism and the overcoming of "housewife feminism."

Notes

1. This essay is based partly on my article, "Shufu feminism wo koete—Post 55-nen taisei no josei shutai e," in Issue 38 of *Shiso to Gendai* (Kashiwa Shoten), so please refer to this essay.

2. Kato Shuichi, Sakamoto Katsumi, and Sechi Yamakaku, eds., *Feminism Collection*, Vol. 3 (Keiso Shobo); Amano Masako, Inoue Teruko, Ueno Chizuko, and Ehara Yumiko, eds., *Nihon no Feminism*, Vol. 8 (Iwanami Shoten).

3. The basis for this labeling of the postwar patriarchal system as a "corporate-centered, lifestyle regulation model," can be found in report of the "women and human rights" workshop of the First East Asian Women's Forum.

4. Hints on the naming of "feminism within administration" (*gyosei sangagata feminism*) came from Nakamura Yoichi's essay "Feminism to shakai system," in *Feminism no mezasu shakai*, compiled by Kanai Yoshiko (Kanagawa Josei Center), as well as with discussions I had with the author. The point has been raised, which involves the "housewife feminism" nature of Japanese feminism, that the establishment of study and training seminars by local government bodies has led to the establishment of rules for appointments of women to commissions and committees and has thus led to the creation of a kind of "citizens in government pay," and that this does not in any way lead to what has been seen as the tasks for Japanese society, namely the building of an autonomous citizen sector and the cultivation of people to play a coordinating role in this process. Issues such as the right to abortion and reproductive self-determination, which are indispensable for the creation of women's labor rights and sexual autonomy have been neglected as the participation of women

in political bodies and administration has been promoted, and this has led to no more than a preservation of the "corporate warrior plus housewives" system.

5. Claudia von Welhof, Maria Mies and Veronika Bennholdt-Thomsen, eds., *Sekai System to Josei*, translated by Furuta Mutsumi and Yoshimoto Yuko (Fujisawa Shoten).

6. The record of this debate can be found in Nihon Josei Kenkyu-kai, eds., *Feminism ha doko e iku* (Shokado).

7. In addition to note 5, Mary Mahler, *Kyokaisen wo yaburu!—Ecofeminism shakai shugi ni mukatte*, translated by Jufuku Mami and Goto Hiroko (Shinhyoron), and other works.

8. For some intensive results of Japanese Marxist feminism, see Ueno Chizuko, *Kafuchosei to shihonsei* (Iwanami Shoten).

9. Ehara Yumiko, *Radical feminism saiko, Sochi to shite no seishihai* (Keiso Shobo).

10. Shiota Sakiko, "Genzai feminism to nihon no shakai seisaku," in Joseigaku Kenkyukai, eds., *Joseigaku to Seiji Jissen* (Keiso Shobo).

11. Iwamoto Misako, "Seishoku no jiko ketteiken to nihonteki seisaku kettei," in *Joseigaku*, the journal of the Nihon Joseigakkukai.

12. Documentation of the spread of the "Agnes debate" in Japan can be found in *Agnes* (JICC Kan).

13. For a compilation of the criticisms leveled during the 1990s against the "withdrawal theory," which engulfed many feminists, see Ogura Toshimaru and Ohashi Yukako, eds., *Hataraku/hatarakanai feminism* (Seikyusha).

14. This opposition was schematized by Hatatani Minoru in "Jinken-ron no shatei," in *Nenpo sabetsuron kenkyu*. For discussion on the debate within women's studies of human rights and feminism, see the record of the symposium entitled "80-nendai feminism wo sokatsu suru," in *Joseigaku nenpo* (no. 12).

15. Ernesto Laclau and Chantal Mouffe, *Post-marx-shugi to seiji—kongenteki minshushugi no tame ni*, translated by Yamazaki Kaoru and Ishizawa Takeshi (Omura Shoten).

16. Femilogue no kai, eds., *Femilogue* (Genbunsha), (four issues have been published so far).

17. Debate between Ueno Chizuko and Hanazaki Kohei, "Minority no shiso to shite no feminism," in *Jokyo* (October/November 1992). One of the foci of this debate was the reactions from the feminist side to a statement by Hanazaki, a pro-feminist, local people's movement theorist. He stated that, "I see feminism as asking for a rice ball under a blue sky, rather than for steak in the smog. In other words, it rejects the attainment of modernist concepts (such as asking for progress and development, prosperity and participation in political bodies), and calls rather for ecological values such as people's solidarity." The reactions to this were that he was pushing this view onto feminism, that it was for feminism itself to decide such issues. For instance, "We'd like to eat both rice balls and steak under a blue sky." If this is impossible, however, both "steak in the smog" and "rice balls under a blue sky" might be possible choices. In any case, this choice has to be made by feminism itself. For the time being, feminism faces the necessity of having a two-tiered or three-tiered

strategy. Feminism has thus found itself forced to be purposefully theoretically self-contradictory.

18. For instance, the discussion between Hanazaki Kohei and Kondo Keiko in *Yu*, the newsletter of the Sapporo Freedom School.

19. Kano Mikiyo (a proponent of the forementioned withdrawal theory), "Guntai e no sankanyuron," in *Risky business shihonshugi* (no. 5 of the *New Feminism Review* series, April 10, 1994, Gakuyo Shobo).

2

The Women's Movement: Progress and Obstacles

Dialogue with Kitazawa Yoko, Matsui Yayori, and Yunomae Tomoko

Matsui: This year is a very important one, as we must reflect upon the 50 years that have passed since the end of World War II. Considering the women's movement specifically, I think there were problematic points from the very beginning. Women who collaborated with the wartime regime, in such groups as the Greater Japan Women's Patriotic Association (Dai-Nippon Aikoku Fujin-kai), an organization set up to incorporate women into Japan's war effort, were later reincorporated into society without any reflection upon what they had done.

Because the emancipation of women was taken very seriously by the U.S. occupation forces, a new women's movement emerged, including progressive groups connected with, for instance, the Japan Communist Party (JCP), which had been repressed during the war but emerged as a strong force in the immediate postwar years.

With the beginning of the Cold War, however, the U.S. authorities felt increasingly threatened by the democratic women's movement and by progressive forces in general. As a result, there was an effort to revive the community groups associated with the old Patriotic Association, and its leaders were, after formal "re-education," restored to leadership status within their communities.

In consequence, two kinds of groups existed at that time: the conservatives, whose roots harked back to the war days, and the progressive forces seeking emancipation from feudalistic discrimination, as represented by the Japan Women's Democratic Club (Fujin Minshu Club), whose formation had been encouraged by the American authorities at Douglas MacArthur's GHQ. At the core of this second group, though, were the progressive political parties and the women's sections of the labor unions.

In 1955, the progressive forces coalesced into two coalitions under the influence of the JCP, the Central Conference of Working Women (Hataraku Fujin no Chuo Shukai) and the Japanese Mothers' Congress (Hahaoya Taikai); but later, with the increasing distance between the JCP and Japan Socialist Party, the women's movement failed to make advances in the post-1960 period.

Women Speak Out—Being a Woman Is Wonderful

With the dawn of the 1970s, however, a new wave called Women's Lib swept in. The influence of the United States was certainly important, but the Japanese Lib movement was not a simple import. In contrast to the progressive women's groups that operated under the umbrellas of the political parties and the conservative community groups that acted as instruments of the ruling political system, Women's Lib was the birth of a movement where women spoke of their liberation in their own words and acted freely. The progressive postwar women's movement can be roughly divided into the pre-1970 and post-1970 periods.

The progressive groups that emerged prior to the 1970s do not seem to have taken on women's issues in the real sense of the term. They gave priority to concepts such as class struggle, political action, and the rights of workers, but were unenthusiastic about issues that related specifically to women. Many people accused the Women's Lib movement of being bourgeois and of being a bit backward. These earlier movements also emphasized changes in conditions. For instance, the women's sections in labor unions called for menstruation and maternity leave, but they seem to have neglected problems and consciousness inherent to women, such as the structure of sexual discrimination and sexuality.

The 1970s, therefore, saw the emergence of a whole new type of women's liberation movement. I myself was one of the founders of the Women's Lib group called the WLF Group (WLF no Kai). Because Japanese society is so male-centered, there was always a lot of anger among women, but there was also a strategy of avoiding women's issues that women followed in order to work in this men's world. I myself worked as a newspaper reporter, and for the first ten years of my career I avoided dealing with women's issues. In fact, I resented the fact that I was a woman, and tried to deny it as I lived my life.

The message from the Women's Lib movement that "being a woman is wonderful" was revolutionary for me. I began to feel positive about the fact that I was a woman.

Raising Women's Sexuality

Yunomae: The women's issues that would remain central years later, such as sex and sexuality, emerged suddenly in the 1970s. It certainly seems that the waves of economic growth and sexual liberation occurred simultaneously, and that in this sense there were areas of progress. However, this did not translate into personal sexual choice for women. For instance, on the issue of reproductive health and rights, women organized to oppose the revision of the Eugenics Protection Act.

In the 1980s, the problem of violence against women emerged, with the establishment of the Rape Assistance Center and Ochiai Keiko's novel *The Rape*. The establishment of the Center, in particular, was very meaningful. It was in the late 1980s that personal sexual choice assumed a central position in the women's movement. Radical feminism emerged during this period, and with it women began to seriously tackle the issues of sexual harassment and violence. The lesbian movement also began to take shape.

The period from the late 1980s to early 1990s was very interesting. We saw the emergence of the antipornographic advertising and antibeauty contest movements, as well as a long series of incidents involving sexual violence. Women have protested against the treatment the mass media has given to these, but it seems that they represent, ironically, a backlash among men against the stronger voices gained by women.

As we entered the 1990s, violence against children, the *jugun ianfu,* or "comfort women," and wife-beating emerged as issues in the women's movement. In addition, a spate of incidents involving murders and other crimes by foreign women in Japan have made the headlines. These women, who were traditionally victims, suddenly turned around and committed crimes. In any case, violence against women has begun to come out into the open.

The issues of women's health and bodies remain important, and women's clinics continue to operate. Menopause has also been taken up, in positive terms, as something to accept as natural.

Women in Social Movements

Matsui: In rough terms, we can paint the overall picture as follows: The major women's groups formed in both the prewar and postwar periods are organized into a federation, in the form of the 52 groups which make up the Liaison Group for the Implementation of the Resolution from the International Women's Year Conference of Japan (Kokusai Fujin-nen Renraku-kai). In addition to these, however, are the groups with a clear feminist perspective which have emerged since Women's Lib. There are also groups which are not women's movement groups, but which deal with social issues from a women's perspective, but I would like to let Kitazawa Yoko speak about those.

Kitazawa: I would like to say something about the role that women have played in the citizens' and social movements. Matsui Yayori mentioned the Central Conference of Working Women and the Mothers' Congress earlier, but I would like to point out another movement in which women took the major initiative: the movement to ban hydrogen and nuclear bombs. Like the Mothers' Congress this was a peace movement, but it eventually became wrapped up in the struggle for leadership between the JCP and SDPJ. On the surface it appears that the movement retreated with the growing distance between the two progressive parties, but I think that we can find value in the activities that women carried out inside it.

Grassroots Women—Japan and the Third World

Until the 1970s, it was typical for Japanese women to play a supporting role in the peace and citizens' movements. The Women's Lib movement was certainly stimulated by what was happening in the United States, but we cannot forget what was happening in Japan at the time, namely, the anti-Vietnam War movement, and the movements at Sanrizuka, against the construction of an international airport, and Kita-Fuji, against a Self-Defense Force base. Here women did not simply play the supporting role they had in the anti-nuclear bomb movement, but acted independently. I think the difference can be found in the prescription for social change issued by the Women's Action Squad (Fujin Kodo Butai) at Sanrizuka. They fought along with the men, to be sure, but it was astounding that they developed their own strategy to work for social change. This was what was happening at the grassroots levels of Japanese society in the 1970s.

In this sense, the things taking place in Japan had more similarities with the movements of Asia than they did with their European counterparts. I think there are many similarities between the styles of fighting of women in Sanrizuka and liberation struggles in Asia or the third world. The Japanese Women's Lib movement was stimulated by the people in the United States, but it was not a simple import. From a woman's point of view, there were many similarities between Japan and the third world. This was a special characteristic of what happened here.

Women's Initiatives Toward Self-Governance

As we entered the 1980s, we saw the emergence of the anti-synthetic detergent movement, consumer groups such as the Seikatsu Club Cooperative, and the anti-nuclear power movement, which was given stimulus by the Chernobyl disaster. In earlier times these women would probably have been incorporated into political movements led by men, but a special feature of the 1980s is that they acted independently.

When we speak of citizens, we are faced with the fact that most men do not typically live in their towns during the day and cannot thus be considered citizens. It is only at night that they return home. As a result, it is women who tend to become involved in local issues. At present, however, these local groups are not specifically women's groups and are not involved in issues such as sexual harassment. I think one problem for us to consider is how the relationship between these two kinds of groups can be strengthened. Ties cannot be created mechanically, so I think it has to come from a development of the different movements.

Looking elsewhere, I think the movement to buy bananas directly from the Philippines rather than from the plantations run by multinational corporations is a specifically Japanese phenomenon. Women travel to the Philippines on study tours, share experiences with the farmers there, and as a result find their ways of thinking changed. Men are hardly involved at all. The possibility of people going across borders to create solidarity with their counterparts in the South really exists among women. In Zushi City, for instance, the women's self-governing movement started as something merely to protect a forest, but they eventually took on issues such as the U.S. bases in Japan and the Japan-U.S. Security Treaty. Women eventually went directly to Washington, DC, to negotiate with the U.S. government.

It is true that women participate very little in Japanese national politics, but they are very much involved in local issues. Politics are changing as a result of this. Citizen's movements led by women are very much involved in self-governance.

Consciousness of Japan's Aggression

Matsui: I think it is in the peace and environmental movements that Japanese women really demonstrated their power during the postwar period. The largest streams within the peace movement were the anti-nuclear bombs and the anti-U.S. military base movements. Both of these were based on a victim mentality, however, and this was a serious limitation. The issues of war responsibility and the economic invasion of Asia were never adequately addressed. There were reasons in Korea itself for the fact that the issue of "comfort women," or military sex slaves, was not addressed until recently, but I think there is a need for us to reflect upon the question of why it was not addressed in Japan.

Even among women there are strong reactions against the idea of Japan having been an aggressor nation. In the Japan country report I prepared for the East Asian Women's Forum, which was held in Enoshima in October 1994, I used the phrase "the lack of consciousness of aggression," but had to delete it because of the strong objections of the women in the 52 groups. The phrase "there were war collaborators even among the postwar women's movement" also had to be taken out. Mentioning this notion is still a taboo for conservatives.

The environmental protection movement spread throughout the country in the beginning of the 1970s, with its roots in the antipollution struggles. This is because the mothers of the victims of Minamata Disease (mercury poisoning by the Chisso chemical company) and women in local communities became a major force which was rooted in their communities. As Kitazawa Yoko said, women see things differently from men. Men are tied up in the corporate society, but women are alienated from it, and it is easier for them to see the evils these corporations carry out. In this sense, the environmental protection movement is also linked to the anti-nuclear power movement on the 1980s. What was lacking here, as well, was a type of thinking that went beyond national borders. For instance, women in residents' movements seem to have very little awareness of the issue of pollution exports.

Besides their work in the peace movement and antipollution struggles, women also contributed to the emergence of NGOs working on third world issues in the late 1980s, and they were very active here as well.

War and Sexuality—The "Comfort Women" Issue

Kitazawa: I'd like to discuss the issue of "comfort women" a little further. For a long time in Japan, the issue of war and sexuality was taboo, and this taboo was broken by the women's movement. It was first made an issue by Korean women and quickly became a political problem. There were many other war issues which remained unresolved, but none of them entered the political arena. The issue of "comfort women" became popular, and, as a result, other issues were taken up. This was a result of women's power.

Matsui: In the 1970s, the issue of "comfort women" was brought up by Korean women involved in the opposition movement to Kieseng tourism. During that period South Korea was under dictatorship, however, and because of the energy spent on the anti-dictatorship struggle there was simply no room to take up the "comfort women" problem. As we moved into the 1990s, however, the women's movement there began to take on the issue head on, and victims started speaking out for the first time. Japanese women began to cooperate with them, and the issue thus moved onto the international stage.

Yunomae: In order for the former "comfort women" to be able to speak out about their experiences, it was necessary to have a ready audience. It was with the rise of the Korean women's movement that this audience emerged. I think this was encouraged by the international movement, which says that it is OK to speak out about sexuality and about violence against women.

Kitazawa: The issue of "comfort women" thus moved into the Japanese political arena, and in the end the government was forced to recognize its involvement. The movement for Japan to offer apologies to its Asian neighbors has become stronger with this. I think it is because of women's power that issues such as the "comfort women," which were ignored for nearly 50 years, have now become political issues.

Differing Opinions among Japanese Women

Matsui: We must remember, however, that the government's present position is that the issues such as the "comfort women" were resolved with the offering of reparations under bilateral treaties. It completely refuses to change this position. Why? I think that one reason has to do with Japanese women themselves. One of the major forces opposing the resolution of the "comfort women" issue and postwar compensation is composed of groups such as the Senyukai (Veterans' Society) and Izokukai (Bereaved Families' Association), whose members were deeply involved in the war. Many of the members are women who lost their sons or husbands during the war. In addition to being a major pillar of the Liberal Democratic Party, which was the ruling party throughout most of Japan's postwar period, they represent a strong power by themselves, and they oppose postwar compensation and any resolution of the "comfort women" issue. We thus cannot simply say that women oppose war; we must consider the roots of these thoughts.

At the East Asian Women's Forum, there were women's groups who were concerned about the fact that the Japanese government would be unhappy to see us take up the issue of "comfort women." Some women's groups said they would be unable to work with us if we took up that issue. They welcomed our doing it, but just said we could not do it together.

One of the things that concerns me as we approach the Beijing Conference is that many women's groups are expressing the hope that nongovernmental organizations and the government will cooperate. In my opinion, we need to make it clear that our position is different from that of the government and that there are areas in which we simply cannot cooperate.

Yunomae: Whether we look at the "comfort women" issue or the problem of female foreign workers in Japan, we see that the problems are becoming international. Some people do not seem to understand that Japan's problems are in fact international.

Kitazawa: There are also women who do not want to confront the problems of human rights and of violence against women. They are willing to take up the question of equality in abstract terms, but are not really able to deal with the issues raised by feminists. I think they refuse to confront these problems because they imply the necessity of becoming independent. It is in this sense that women do not really have independence within social movements.

Reaction in Japanese Society

Matsui: "Empowerment" has recently become a keyword meaning that women have to take on the power to act. In this sense, however, it seems to me that Asian women have a great deal of power, and it is precisely the Japanese women who are the most dispossessed of all within the region. What percentage of people participating in women's or social movements are women, and are their numbers increasing? If we look at young Japanese women, we see that any interest they might have had in social issues has been destroyed by a conformist educational system, material affluence, and a culture of mass consumption. I don't think we can say they are "empowered" in any way.

Yunomae: I think the problem of sexual violence did not surface until the 1980s because taking up this issue means, at least temporarily, confronting men. Many people react negatively to this. It seems that women have tried to avoid this whenever possible. If this is true, then I think this represents something special which we can label Japanese feminism.

Matsui: If we look at the issue of "women's independence" historically, we see that up until the 1970s this mainly meant economic independence, or the right to work. When women began to demand sexual independence, however, the pressure brought against them by men increased suddenly. For instance, my male reporter colleagues at the newspaper I worked for began to look at me differently after I took up the issue of sex tours. Men do not necessarily react negatively to the idea of the right to work or of equality at work, but when the issue of sexuality is taken up they react bitterly.

Yunomae: It seems that men feel that the basis of their existence is being threatened. I do not know if they are conscious of this or not.

Matsui: The clear difference between the pre- and post-Women's Lib eras, however, is the problem of sexuality, and that women began to question the everyday relationships they had with men. I think this was a fundamental break. The difficulty facing Japanese feminism is that, regardless of whether men react against it or simply ignore it, they do not recognize that sexual discrimination is a major ideological problem. The Japanese men we call "intellectuals" show a surprising lack of understanding about feminism, and this is deeply rooted in Japanese society. I really wonder what we will have to do to change this.

Kitazawa: Another way men react to the problem of sexual discrimination is to grin as they speak about it. They seem serious when discussing racial discrimination, but even men who call themselves feminists tend to grin when talking about gender.

Matsui: In Japan, the consciousness gap between men and women has only widened. Women have changed a lot in the past

20 years, but what about men? I think therefore that the problems have to be confronted together with men, though some people say that this is wishful thinking.

The Women's Movement at a Crossroads

Kitazawa: One thing I find very Japanese about the preparations for the coming Beijing Conference is that local authorities are lending their support. This is both good and bad. Local authorities means local governments, and they therefore operate on tax money, and they believe that tax monies have to be shared fairly among all citizens. The problem arising from this is that they will not necessarily send women who can make women's issues clear or who can really represent women's interests.

Matsui: At present, women's sections in local governments are really energetic, and there are many well-equipped women's centers being built. Many of the women connected to this, however, are conservatives, and some of them were involved in the war effort. There are instances in many areas where members of the conservative local women's club (Fujin-kai) actually show hostility toward feminist women.

Kitazawa: There are instances, however, where people trying to build shelters come to ask for assistance from local administrations. This is because the local authorities act as a sort of office for their communities. They do not, however, have facilities to resolve problems. As a result, the private women's groups try to resolve the problems themselves. It is a bizarre relationship, since many of the women's groups are simply doing things they believe the government should be doing. We have to sever this relationship.

Matsui: Recently I was surprised to go to a local city and find that there were no independent women's groups at all, that the old women's club was all that existed.

Kitazawa: Yes, tax money is used for these groups, and it is these women who are going to be sent to Beijing. Very little money is given to those who really need to go or to the foreign women who have been brought to Japan to work.

Government Proposals for "Joint Participation"

Yunomae: The administration of women's affairs has reached an impasse because it is difficult to attract participation if only women's issues are emphasized. As a result, the administrators have begun to use ideas such as "coexistence between men and women," or "joint participation." Changing men is important, yes, but I can't help but feel that they are leaving important elements out.

Kitazawa: I think these very ideas of "coexistence" or "equal participation" are themselves mistaken. How can we have coexistence if we don't have equality? Men are fond of using slogans such as "coexistence between men and women," or "coexistence with Asia," but I don't understand how un-equals can coexist. One gets the distinctive impression that they are looking downward. They probably believe that affirmative action is a ludicrous idea.

Yunomae: I think the idea of "equal participation" is good if it means sharing in policy-making, but the slogan "coexistence" hits me the wrong way. I feel resistance to it. It seems to be simply hanging a veil over the existence of inequality.

Kitazawa: When women get married and have children, they have to leave their jobs. All women get to taste some such grief. And women feel irritated as they raise children. They feel, on the one hand that they want to escape from the situation but, on the other hand, their way of looking at the world changes, and they become interested in food and in what is happening in the rest of Asia. As a result they end up going to the women's affairs administration because it is the only place they can find to explore these interests. The problem is that they need to go beyond just studying, and to take action.

Are Japanese Women Empowered?

Kitazawa: I really doubt that we can say that Japanese women have been empowered. If you ask where Japanese society is changing, however, I would answer that it is women who are changing. Women change and, by doing so, change the whole society around them. The pattern of women exerting themselves silently persists, but a process is beginning whereby women in social movement propose new issues to be dealt with.

Yunomae: Sexual discrimination is very strong in Japan, and I think it is supported by the sexual division of labor here. At present, over half of women approve of the sexual division of labor (for men it's over 60%), compared to over 70% just 20 years ago. What remains unchanged, however, is that this figure is much higher than in other developed countries. I think the problem of sexuality is also something which is still difficult to deal with, and so is the lack of empowerment. I think it will be even harder to get the percentage of women approving of the sexual division of labor down below 50%, because reaching this will mean a real change in Japanese society.

Matsui: Thinking on prostitution is also very diverse. Have there been any changes in men's perceptions on buying sex? I have been involved in this issue since the 1970s, with the Kieseng tourism issue, but the sex tours continue, the sex industry has only gained influence, and we have to ask ourselves whether anything has changed. It seems that our campaign has been ineffective. The terrible instances of violence directed against Thai women who have been trafficked into the sex industry are commonplace occurrences in this society. I wonder how we will be able to change this commodification of female sexuality.

On the other hand, the idea of prostitution as a free job choice is spreading internationally. What, we have to ask ourselves, is the substance of personal choice on sexuality and sexual independence? If the empowerment of women means their reaching economic, psychological, and sexual autonomy, then it seems to me that sexual autonomy has become very difficult in the context of commercialism.

Another difficult issue to confront is, empowerment for what? I am suspicious about the American model of empowerment, which means the right to grasp for power just as men do. We have to look for an empowerment that doesn't mean becoming corporate warriors just like men. Everybody says that we need alternatives. Now we have to imagine what exactly these alternatives will be.

3

The Movement Today:
Difficult but Critical Issues

Dialogue with Ehara Yumiko,
Nakajima Michiko, Matsui Yayori,
and Yunomae Tomoko

Nakajima: The term "corporate society" is used quite often today. It means a society where the greatest value is placed on corporate development, and one which supports the lifestyles and families of men working in corporations. It means a society where all living is meant to support the economic growth of corporations. It is under such a social system that Japan became an economic superpower and began its economic invasion of the rest of Asia.

Job opportunities for new female college graduates have become a major problem recently, but it is not a question of the recession ending up hurting female students. It is rather that the recession brought out the true features of Japanese corporate society.

The fact that our corporate society rests upon a foundation of sexual discrimination has been well documented. Sexual discrimination exists both at the workplace and within the family. In the family, women alone bear the burden of housework and by doing so sustain the corporate warriors. In the workplace, the structure of wages demonstrates the structure of discrimination: women act as a low-paid, insecure workforce. In other words, the Japanese workplace has a double structure of discrimination. The workplace combines with the family to support the structure of the Japanese corporate society.

The Equal Employment Opportunity Law (EEOL) was enacted in 1985, but in the end was not able to change this corporate society. I am one of those who believed we should try to use this law, and I still believe we should. Unfortunately, however, the behavior demonstrated by firms since the passage of the law not only fails to conform to its goals, but in many cases actually opposes the law's intent.

Two concrete examples of this are the "career-track system" and the use of part-time labor. The "track system" was instituted as a way of preserving sexual discrimination while at the same time putting up a facade that there was actually equality. The work traditionally performed by men was labeled the *sogo shoku*, or "managerial track," and only an extremely small number of women were allowed to enter it. The work traditionally done by women was simply relabeled *ippan shoku*, or the "general clerical track."

In regard to part-timers, the percentage of women in the workforce is surely increasing, but many are working part-time, and the labor conditions they face are steadily deteriorating. The wage gap is growing larger. Large supermarkets are encouraging short-hour part-time work as a means of cutting wages.

In this way, the corporate society is becoming stronger in regard to sexual discrimination. In addition, changes in the industrial structure are making the labor market more fluid, and this concerns men as well as women. I believe that this situation, however, gives us the opportunity to consider alternatives. At present, however, I am afraid that both the labor movement and the women's movement are not doing a good job of considering how to use this chance to change people's lifestyles. As a result, the labor force is becoming liquid in a way that benefits only corporate efficiency.

I would like to talk about how the women's movement is responding to this by discussing movements surrounding the EEOL. If we look at the number of participants and the level of discussion, we can say that interest in this issue peaked in the early 1980s. This turned into a debate among women who were interested in labor over the question of "protection versus equality," and the women were split. They were not able to forge any linkages with the women's movement or the movement called feminism.

If we think about why this was so, we can say, first, that there are problems within the labor movement itself, mainly in the idea of "workism," or the obligation of work, which says that women can be liberated through labor.

The Problem of Maternal Protection

Within the women's labor movement, an even greater problem is the idea of "maternal protectionism," or the idea that women need special legal protection because of the role they play as mothers. Some people claim that "the greatest need that working women face is maternity protection." In concrete terms, this means requests for maternal leave, menstruation leave, and the preservation of regulations limiting overtime and late night labor. Menstruation leave, in particular, is symbolic of this line of thinking.

There have not yet been any proposals to eliminate maternity leave, but the main attacks from business circles over the idea of "protection versus equality" in the new law have come in the areas of menstruation leave and limits on overtime and late night work.

The women in the women's labor movement who support this position insist that nothing that deviates at all from these ideas be accepted. The idea that "equality" should be abandoned because it would mean having these gains taken away has led to the split in the movement over "equality" versus "protection."

In regard to other branches of the women's movement outside

of labor, I think that there has been skepticism toward the concepts of "labor" and "equality." We can find examples of this among people who place a great focus on "everyday life" (*seikatsu*), ecologists, and people whose main focus is to put into question the growth strategy of corporations. In the feminist movement there are even people who have no interest at all in removing sexual discrimination from the workplace. As a result, we were given the EEOL made to measure for the business world. This is why we really need to find alternatives.

In Germany, with the exception of a few jobs, work on Sundays and holidays is forbidden. Recently, however, these regulations have been relaxed as they were seen as impediments to international competitiveness. The decision was that labor standard offices could grant permission for work on Sundays if this was deemed necessary to retain international competitiveness. When questioned about this decision, a government official said that, "In Japan working on Sundays is considered normal, so we have to change to be able to compete with them." We can see, therefore, that the poor working conditions and sexual discrimination in Japan are pulling down working conditions in Europe, especially those of working women. The effect is not just on Europe, of course; Asian workers are being hurt as well.

I feel, therefore, that as long as Japanese women continue to be victims in Japan they will add to the oppression of Asian women. I believe that creating solidarity with women in Asia and around the world means changing the structure of discrimination within Japanese labor.

Equality Both at Home and at Work

In order to do this, the idea of "equality both at home and at work" is very important. Concretely speaking, this means shortening the working hours of men and changing their working patterns. In principle, at least, the Ministry of Labor has found itself forced to accept this, since it is planning to ratify ILO Convention No. 156 concerning Equal Opportunities and

Equal Treatment for Men and Women Workers with Family Responsibilities.

Ehara: I also believe this is where we need to go. The people from the *seikatsu* (everyday life) or ecological tendencies tend to reject participation in labor, or to criticize this as an ideology of economic growth, without thinking about how the women's movement should relate to the labor movement. When considering women's issues, for instance, we find that even women who are not corporate warriors are affected by corporate society by having their livelihoods, environment, and bodies invaded. The fact that workplaces are made male-oriented through sexual discrimination prevents the voicing of opinions to solve problems involving women's bodies. Even for people who believe that they must protect themselves or take care of their own environment, labor is an issue that must be dealt with. In this sense I think we can find weaknesses in the women's movement.

At the same time, I think that the "maternal protectionism" that one finds in the labor movement is a big problem. For people involved in issues such as bodies, sexuality, and sexual violence, maternity, though natural, is not sacred and involves social constructs. They understand that it is impossible to build a movement based on the idea of protecting maternity and that they must fight for the ability to make their own decisions in regards to their own bodies. I think, therefore, that if people in the labor movement created an alliance with the women's movement, they would be able to overcome the tendency of simply trying to shorten working hours and prevent overtime in the name of protecting motherhood.

Matsui: In regard to equality, of course, there is also the American-style way of thinking, which says that women should carry guns and march alongside men in the army. I was surprised when I attended a mass media conference held in Washington, D.C., to find people advocating the idea that women should compete to obtain top positions in society, as company presidents, politicians, or whatever. It seems that women in the media are eager to talk about how to obtain power, but they ignore the problems of women workers in the field. I really wonder what this kind of equality means.

I personally do not place much value on the idea of equality itself, and only see it as a means. The more important question to ask is, equality for what?

This also relates to the idea of participation. People often speak about political participation, but the reality is that the only women who act like men in the present political system today are those who are acceptable to men. Unless we emphasize the need to change politics itself, I will remain suspicious about the idea of participation.

Nakajima: Why is it that when we speak about equality we are always accused of seeking American-style equality? In Japan today, there are not that many women who rule over other women in oppressive ways.

Matsui: Isn't it a difference in the idea of how to give power to women? I think it is better if there is a diversity of roads to follow, such as entering the power structure or trying to shake it from the outside.

Ehara: What is most important is not to prevent people from taking other approaches, but to encourage them and to harmonize our efforts. I think the biggest problem is that we don't have the concept of working in the different ways we can instead of opposing one another.

The Right of Sexual Self-Determination

Yunomae: As we entered the 1980s the problem of sexuality came to the surface, in particular after 1989 with the emergence of campaigns against sexual harassment and pornography. Uno Sosuke, the prime minister at that time, was forced to resign because of a scandal involving a woman, something that was virtually unheard of. In the same year, a large number of women won seats in the Upper House elections, giving women an unprecedented visibility.

Compared to that time, however, our energy level has ebbed.

Nakajima: The upsurge around 1989 had something to do with the limits placed on expression. At the same time, a new type of thinking about prostitution was emerging in Europe, one that favored its liberalization. The situation became such that it was impossible to put up resistance by using the old idea that "the commodification of sex is evil." As a result, a new way of thinking became necessary for those taking on the issue of sexuality.

Yunomae: I believe that the idea of sexual self-determination came out from inside the movement, but I think that historically and socially limits had to be placed on it. The question of what kind of sexual self-determination we are seeking is never made clear.

Ehara: I don't think we have a clear enough idea of under what circumstances that self-determination should be restricted.

Nakajima: The biggest problem here is prostitution. Since people say that the choice to sell sex for money is a personal one, I was very surprised to see people say that this falls under the idea of sexual self-determination.

Matsui: The real dividing line here is whether or not one thinks of performing sex in exchange for money as a form of labor. Internationally, there is one stream of thought that the right to sell sex is a human right. In Japan, most feminists oppose prostitution because it is a system of treating women not as human beings but as mere commodities, but we are strongly opposed to discrimination against women in prostitution.

If we accept prostitution, then we will become unable to oppose sex tours, an activity which we have carried out since the 1970s. It would be contradictory to say that prostitution is acceptable and then condemn men for going on sex tours.

Nakajima: Under the Convention on the Elimination of All Forms of Discrimination Against Women, it is only forced prostitution that is clearly outlawed. It is difficult to think about where we should go from here. I believe that sexual self-determination does not exist when power, including direct force, of course, but psychological and economic power as well, is involved in the decision-making process. Therefore, I only thought this principle applied to cases where no money is involved, when the only criterion for decision-making is what one does and does not like. Recently, however, some people have begun to claim that receiving money should also be a personal choice.

Ehara: The problem is really whether selling sex for money fits into the principle of sexual self-determination. It goes without saying that everybody is opposed to prostitution when it is coerced and when it goes against the free will of the person who is involved. Then the question is, should we accept prostitution when there is no coercion involved?

One of the factors behind the emergence of this debate is that without recognizing prostitution as labor we cannot speak of the exploitation involved. If prostitution is simply labeled as a crime, then it is impossible to speak about exploitation. In Japan, for instance, prostitution itself can be the target of prosecution, so if a woman makes a free contract to sell sex, and the terms of the contract are not respected by the other party, she has no way of seeking remedy.

Why Is Prostitution a Female Profession?

Matsui: Fundamentally, this has to do with the question of how we view sexuality. It is clear that views on sexual activities and sexuality are becoming more diverse. What I fear, however, is that people will assume that Western views on human rights are advanced, and will come to accept the European tendency to legalize prostitution as an advanced type of thinking.

At present, people say that forced prostitution as well as child prostitution should be banned. But I think it's very difficult to draw a line, to say that up to the age of 18 it's wrong but that after that it's acceptable. It is not easy to distinguish between free and forced prostitution in the third world because most prostituted women are forced there by poverty.

Ehara: That line needs to be drawn, however. When we discuss the issue of sexual self-determination, we have to consider the question of what to do for minors. Even if we allow for the legalization of selling sex, the problems remain of who should administer this "freedom" and whether the purchasing side should be legalized. If we don't make decisions on these matters, it's hard to predict what will happen. What should be done for people who are incapable of making such decisions?

Matsui: On the other hand, however, we have to confront the problem of why it is just women who work as prostitutes. At present there is an uneven power relationship between men and women, so women need to earn money through prostitution. In the future, if the relationship becomes equal, I wonder if the situation will continue where one side pays money to the other.

In Europe, women hardly question men at all in their debates. There is almost no discussion on what people think of the fact the men shell out the money for women to perform sex.

Ehara: I think that the logic and behavior of those who buy sex cannot easily be legitimized. For instance, people say it is a way of having sex without the woman becoming pregnant. But sex and procreation cannot be so completely delinked. There is a fundamental problem if one sees these actions in such clear isolation.

In addition, even when people who sell sex say it is all right, it is completely different than saying that no bad effects come from these sexual activities. It may have negative effects on them. Even if we accept that people are selling sex by their own free will, that does not mean that we have to legitimize the buying of sex in all circumstances.

Even if prostitution is accepted as a right, no one can claim that men be given the right to buy it. But some people oppose restrictions on the right of men to buy sex, saying that this would hinder their own right to sell it.

Yunomae: In the past we have always said that sex was equivalent to personality, but I don't understand this anymore. People in the younger generation feel resistance when people speak of sex in moral tones. I myself feel resistance to the idea that sex is personality. I can really understand the feeling of not wanting to turn sex into such a heavy thing.

Nakajima: It is said that prostitution is unacceptable because it involves the selling of personality, but then we have to ask ourselves, does not everybody sell personality? People in society are all selling it. The debate that ensues concerns why it is only in sex that selling personality is wrong.

Ehara: There is another logic, however, which says that there are many people who put a meaning on sex, and for them harming sexuality means harming personality. We cannot simply ignore these people's reality. But all I'm saying is that it is a strange situation if we can only discuss sexuality in terms of its link to personality. It is strange to legitimize prostitution by thinking that if it's alright for us, it's alright for everybody else.

Matsui: In order to understand the lack of enthusiasm in the anti-pornography movement, we have to look at the strength of the line of thinking which calls for sexual freedom. In Japan, the porno video market is said to be worth ¥10 trillion, which dwarfs the industry in other countries. This is also supported by the rationale that people are doing it freely, and so why not. It is the pornography industry which makes this claim loudest.

Nakajima: That's because we live in a time when the old argument that sex should never be commodified is not accepted.

Ehara: Considering the fact that so many women are involved in this commodification, the women's movement is bound to find itself in a predicament.

Matsui: Those women have internalized the present dominant values in society, in particular the worship of money.

Ehara: They have been taught all along that they will be judged by their sexuality, and those around them feel the same way. At some point, they turn this logic around, and say, well, if I am to be judged by my sexuality, why not use my sexuality as something to give me value. It means the transformation from being seen into showing. I don't think this logic is so far removed from what the women's movement has been saying since the 1970s, and I don't find it so alien. I think there is a need for us to develop a logic through which we can judge this behavior with a common standard. We therefore need to think about the "commodification of sexuality." And I mean together with women who are involved in prostitution.

Matsui: People in the Asian women's movement have recently begun to emphasize spirituality. They are seeking internal things. In Japan, today, everything is external. There is very little interest in the internal. Women are only concerned about appearance, and they feel empty. It seems to be the result of material affluence and the pressure of commercialism.

Ecology and Feminism

Matsui: The Japanese women's movement gained the power to convey a message to the outside world mainly with the peace movement in the 1960s and the antipollution movement of the 1970s. I find that all the movements which derived from the antipollution movement, such as the antinuclear movement, the cooperative union, and the consumer movement, all have a very ecological flavor. Most of these movements, however, are carried out mainly by housewives. The reason for this is that the division of labor based on gender in Japan has led to a situation where men work so much that they have no time to participate in citizen's movements. We are left with the ironic situation in which women who are excluded from mainstream society are the ones leading the movements.

I wonder, however, to what extent these women want to change the traditional gender roles. I think a major limitation of the women's movement today is that women try to promote ecology within the framework of the sexual division of labor, without challenging this system in a feminist way.

On the other hand, the feminist movement has very little consciousness of ecology. In third world countries, women face threats to their very existence with environmental destruction, and have to fight for survival. By involving themselves in movements, they have rediscovered their own femininity and feel that it is women themselves who hold the key to solving the environmental crisis today.

When I come back to Japan after visits to Asia, however, I find a very different situation. The reason for this, it turns out, is that ecological feminism emerged as a single track in Japan, with the idea that men should be involved in technological and cultural pursuits, whereas women should take care of nature and maternity. This has been criticized by feminists as supporting the traditional gender roles.

I think the basic limitation of Japanese feminism today is that it does not have any overall vision to counter the fact that the Japanese economy is based on a structure of discrimination. Women involve themselves very strongly on single issues, but don't have a strong vision of how to change the total structure. For this reason I don't think the awareness of ecological issues is very keen either.

Ehara: Japanese ecofeminism has a very strong tendency to use the concept of nature quite symbolically, and I think this ideological coloring is what caused people to dislike that train of thought. Among men involved in the ecology movement, there was a tendency to paint the roles of men and women as natural. It is certain that within the ecological movement the sexual division of labor was maintained. I think women reacted against this.

Nakajima: What disturbed me about ecofeminism is the question of how one could possibly remake Japan into an ecological society without transforming the workplace. What I am trying to do by fighting for women's labor rights is to change the workplace. We have aimed at changing the present corporate society by allowing seikatsu to enter into the workplace. In this sense there should be a relationship to ecology. But as soon as we mention the idea of labor rights we are criticized for neglecting ecology. Then we clash.

People work locally to change their lifestyle, and people work to change their workplaces to support their lifestyle. We are saying that we have to create a society with "the right to live one's own life, the right to manage one's own life, for both men and women," where labor rights and personal rights can be in balance. I think that there was a weakness in not taking up the right to manage one's own life. But this is where we can find ties to ecology.

Matsui: Another point of difficulty with ecology is the suspicion that it is advocating a return to old times. What Asian women are debating now, however, is how to replace the current developmentalism with alternatives both in terms of content and process. They do not advocate a return to the past. There is a shared consciousness that the present model of development is both inhumane and unecological. We need, therefore, to have more debates on how to build alternatives. Because the development model has been taken to its most extreme form in Japan, there is a need for Japanese women to discuss how to change their own society. This does not mean a return to the past.

Ehara: Within the ecological movement there are people who advocate a return to old times. There are lots of people who see things purely in terms of energy, and who therefore say, in the Edo Period (17th–18th century) they made better use of energy, so let's recreate that time. They don't have any consciousness of women's issues.

Matsui: Fundamentally, the basic problem we are confronting is how to go beyond European modern industrial society and technological civilization.

Nakajima: I am involved in women's labor issues because I want to change our corporate society. This does not only involve women's labor rights, but I want both men and women to recognize the need for labor rights in harmony with an affluent personal lifestyle. In order to create solidarity with Asian women, I think we need to change Japanese labor in order to transform our corporate society.

Yunomae: I would like to look at the problem from the angle of sexuality. It is said that education in Japan provides sexual equality. The content, however, is never questioned. We need to clarify this issue.

Matsui: The year 2000 is the beginning of a new millennium, and there is therefore a sort of fever sweeping the globe which says we have to create a new world. There is an overall consensus that our present society has many problems, and I think we need to think of them in terms of gender, ecology, and North-South issues.

Ehara: I think that ideas involving maternity are a threat to the achievement of women's labor rights. It really changes people when women working in such specialist fields as nursing and teaching are given advice that, "If you work, your children will become delinquent." I don't think we can simply ignore the fact that this kind of advice is being given to working women. The treatment given to women at universities, where they receive their specialist knowledge, is really problematic. The problems of sexuality and maternity cannot be ignored, as they bear a relationship to knowledge. Learning, knowledge, and science are all bastions of control. I would like to work to clarify this situation. Under the sexual division of labor, salaries were only given to men, to which I would like to consider the problems of women's labor, bodies, and environment, as problems of knowledge.

II

Issues Facing Women

4

Economic Development and Asian Women

Matsui Yayori

"It is said that the 21st century will be the century of Asia. Japan has become a global economic power; the NIEs (newly industrialized economies—South Korea, Taiwan, and Hong Kong) have achieved outstanding economic development; China and Macao have accelerating economic growth; and Mongolia is moving toward a market economy.

The economic energy of East Asia is having an impact on the lives of people of the world through the filling of the world market with the wealth and abundance of its products. This emergence of Asia is capturing great interest all over the world.

However, it is questionable whether the current type of economic development based on the free market system improves quality of life, gender equality and the advancement of women. . . . Deeply rooted gender-role divisions limit women's participation in policy decision-making in every sphere including economics, politics, society, education, mass media and culture. We maintain that gender equality is still far from being realized."

This statement comes from the East Asian Women's Declaration, which was adopted at the First East Asian Women's Forum held in Japan in October 1994 in preparation for the 1995 Beijing Women's Conference.

Women in the NIEs—National Borders

Women of Southeast Asia have organized a workshop entitled "Women in NICs, Near NICs, and Aspiring NICs" (NICs, or newly industrializing countries, is equivalent to NIEs) in March 1995 as preparation for Beijing. They recognized a need to examine the impacts of the development process on women's life. In the Asia-Pacific region, where countries have followed a single model of economic development since the end of the Cold War. Some of the issues they pointed out, which concern women in the entire region, were sex tours and trafficking in women, migrant workers working outside of their own countries, changes in gender-based roles in families, the feminization of unemployment and poverty, the influence of war and peace on women, and environmental degradation/industrial pollution/women's health.

International Trafficking in Women

International criticism mounted in the 1970s against Japanese men taking sex tours to other Asian countries. Since the 1980s, however, the problem has changed to one of Asian women being trafficked into Japan. Thai women, as is reported in Chapter 11, have been the greatest victims.

The number of Thai women being sent into Japan's sex industry skyrocketed during the same period that their country's economic growth rate went into double digits. Thailand's economic development model encourages foreign investment, is city-centered, promotes industrialization, and is export oriented. It has widened the gap between rich and poor and between city and countryside. In contrast to the prosperity in Bangkok, life in the rural areas have been impoverished. Many farmers are burdened with unbearable debt and find themselves forced into selling their daughters into the sex industry.

Tourism Promotion and AIDS

In Thailand the promotion of tourism as a means to acquire foreign currency, along with consumerism, has played a key role in the unprecedented growth of prostitution. Along with this, HIV infection has spread at an explosive rate; women have been victimized by the epidemic. It has spread especially quickly among young girls, who are unlikely to have contracted it before they were sold into prostitution. This demand for safe young girls is so strong that girls from neighboring countries such as Burma, Laos, Cambodia and southern China have also become victims.

In fact, trafficking in women and girls has become a serious problem all throughout Asia, where everything has come to be seen as a commodity in the free market economy. Women are being sold from Thailand and the Philippines to Japan, Taiwan, Korea, and Hong Kong; from Bangladesh to Pakistan; from Sri Lanka to the Gulf nations. Trafficking in women for the purpose of organized prostitution has become global, and the victims are becoming younger.

The Meaning of Violence Against Women

Since the UN Decade for Women (1976–85), violence against women has emerged as one of the main themes of women's movements internationally. "Women's human rights " were officially spelled out for the first time in Vienna at the 1993 World Conference on Human Rights, and violence against women became a focus of the debate. The UN Declaration on the Elimination of Violence Against Women was adopted later that year, and in it three categories of violence were described: in the family, in the community and by the state. Trafficking in women, along with rape and sexual harassment, was classified as violence in the community, and governments have been asked to take action.

The international women's movement made a tremendous achievement when it succeeded in getting domestic violence, which was long considered a private matter and therefore neglected, to be considered a serious violation of women's human rights. Violence inflicted by husbands against their wives takes place in every society. Traditionally, however, the public sector has been hesitant to intervene, under the rationale that the problem was a personal matter between the husbands and wives. The thinking was that maltreating people outside the family was a crime, but that harming one's wife was tolerable.

Women in Europe and North America were the first to take up domestic violence as an issue, and we have gotten far enough now that governments have been forced into taking some action. In Asia, in addition to domestic violence in general, traditional and religious practices sometimes act as unique forms of domestic violence against women; in Asia cultures of silence compel women to hide their misery, out of both shame and fear.

The Asian Pacific Regional Conference on Inter-familial Violence

In December 1994, the United Nations International Children's Emergency Fund (UNICEF) held its "Asian-Pacific Regional Conference" in Cambodia on interfamilial violence against women. The reality of violence against women in Asia and measures to combat it were discussed, and plans of action were put forward.

Women are exposed to violence even before they are born, and the violence lasts throughout their lifetimes. In India, where parents are reluctant to have daughters for fear that they will not be able to afford dowries, and in China, where a preference for boys has become magnified by the one-child policy, selective abortions and infanticide are widespread. Girls are subject to sexual abuse, and married women are not safe from violence inflicted upon them by their husbands. In extreme cases, such as dowry-related murders in India, thousands of young wives are burned to death or driven to suicide by greedy husbands. Dowry killing is almost a traditional practice, but the sudden increase in recent years may be a consequence of a rapidly spreading consumerism.

One detailed report from Cambodia illustrates how the legacy of genocide from the Pol Pot era continues to haunt Cambodian society. In some men, the trauma of the massacre is manifested as violence inflicted against their wives. The population imbalance between men and women that emerged from the killings has weakened the position of women in general; there have even been cases of men abusing their wives after meeting new women.

At the end of the conference, the Phnom Penh Declaration was adopted, appealing for the creation of a new society without any form of violence.

Development as Structural Violence

In addition to gender violence, the impact of unequal economic development—a form of structural violence—presents serious problems for women. The Asia Pacific Forum on Women, Law and Development (APWLD) organized a Women's Tribunal in December 1994 at Chulalongkorn University in Thailand. Eight women who were victims of serious human rights violations were invited to give testimony about their experiences, and they used their testimony to question the present model of economic development.

One farmer from northeast Thailand talked about the struggle against the Pak Mun Dam by local farmers. The dam was built despite their protests, and because of the dam they can no longer catch fish to eat. Hundreds of farmers asking for proper compensation were met by police violence at the dam site shortly before the APWLD tribunal.

The farmer concluded her testimony at the tribunal by stating angrily that "men in the village now have to leave the village and earn money elsewhere. Women have been left behind, and are struggling to survive. All we can say to development is a big 'NO.'"

Pak Mun is one of many projects planned along the 4,200-kilometer Mekong River. International financial institutions and multinational corporations are developing resort sites, dams and other big projects, neglecting the needs of local people. As a result, the 50 million or so people living along the Mekong in Thailand, Burma, Vietnam, Laos, Cambodia, and China face the danger of extinction. Some Japanese citizens who are deeply concerned about the Mekong development, in cooperation with people from the affected area, have recently started "Mekong Watch" activities.

The struggle against big dams is gaining momentum in many places such as Narmada in India, Kedung Ombo in Indonesia, and Bakun in Sarawak, Malaysia. Women have played an important role in all these movements.

Rainforest Destruction and Indigenous Women

Similarly, women's power has been the driving force behind protests against the destruction of forests, as can be seen in the Chipko movement in India. Southeast Asia, like Brazil and Central Africa, has many rich rainforests. Unfortunately, however, commercial logging has swept through the Philippines, then Indonesia, and now onto Borneo Island, quickly destroying the rainforests and threatening extinction for indigenous peoples. In addition to Japan, the world's largest importer of timber, the NIEs like Korea and Taiwan have extracted massive volumes of tropical hard wood from Sarawak.

Indigenous people—as entire families, men, women, and children—have struggled against logging by blockading roads. The men have been arrested, and the women left with the struggle for survival. One woman from Sarawak who visited Japan at the invitation of a Japanese NGO working on rainforest protection criticized the wasteful, consumer-oriented lifestyle in Japan, pleading, "Do not cut down any more trees. We cannot survive without our forest. Japanese people make furniture and other items with the trees from our forest, and then discard them without giving it a second thought."

Resort Development for Whom?

The Women's Tribunal also pointed out how indigenous people in Asia and the Pacific have been victimized by rapid economic development. The women from the Cordillera in the Philippines reported on the troubles they faced when they lost their livelihoods due to mine development sponsored by foreign capital.

Another source of hardship for indigenous people is tourist development. As a way of earning foreign currency, ASEAN nations have adopted tourism promotion policies, starting with "Visit Thailand Year" in 1987. Billions of people from the wealthy North have traveled to the countries of the South in search of the four s's—sun, sea, sex, and sports. The numbers of tourists from Japan have increased as well, partly because of the strong yen, reaching 13 million in 1994. For 60 to 70 percent of these travelers, the destination is the Asia-Pacific region. Visitors from the NIEs, and especially Korea and Taiwan, are also increasing rapidly.

For local people, however, tourism brings devastation; they are forced to relocate, the natural environment is destroyed, their culture is commercialized, and prostitution becomes rampant. This kind of tourist development is often financed by international financial institutions, private capital, and ODA (official development assistance) from Japan and other nations. In Hawaii and Guam, most hotels and golf courses have been built with Japanese capital; in Indochina, where tourist development has been promoted along with the free-market economy, Chinese capital from NIEs such as Thailand has played a major role.

In response to this, movements against golf courses have spread throughout Southeast Asia. In Indonesia, for instance, farmers continue to resist the confiscation of their farmlands for a planned golf course. Female farmers have played an active role in this movement. The damage to indigenous peoples living near beaches and in remote mountain areas suitable for resort sites is particularly serious. The Chaorei of Phuket Island, Thailand, the Chamoro of Guam Island, and the "Aborigines" in Taiwan's mountain areas, are some of the peoples whose lands and cultures, which are the source of their identities, are in danger of destruction. Women are also being brought into the sex industry in the resorts. Some indigenous people have begun to organize in order to take control of tourism in their own community and to keep foreign capital at bay.

Shrimp Cultivation and Women

Another shocking testimony at the Women's Tribunal concerned shrimp cultivation in Bangladesh. Shrimp farming has been promoted there under the government's policy to acquire foreign currency and the Structural Adjustment Program imposed by the World Bank, and the southern shore area has been transformed into a large cultivation area.

This change ignited protests among local farmers, whose lands were scheduled to be taken away. In 1991, village women organized a demonstration against the shrimp dealers, who responded by hiring armed personnel. These guards shot one woman to death and injured dozens of others.

Shrimp cultivation has spread along many Asian shores. It destroys mangrove forests, deprives farmers of their lands, and threatens the very survival of local people. For instance, near General Santos, a port town in the southern Mindanao in the Philippines, U.S.-based Dole, an agribusiness multinational, has expanded its shrimp cultivation in the area, driving Islamic Moro fishermen away from their villages in the process. In order simply to survive, many women have gone to Gulf nations as migrant workers, and some have returned, without income, after having suffered sexual abuse and/or nonpayment of wages.

In another case, a plan was created in 1994 to use Japanese ODA to build a modern port to allow for the speedy export of marine products to Japan, and area fishermen were displaced, despite their resistance. One young Moro woman who is now working to organize women in the General Santos area said, "The Ramos administration aims to make the Philippines an NIE by the year 2000. The development of Mindanao is being encouraged in order to fulfill this goal. Due to this policy, anyone trying to work with the poor who suffer from development are met with pressure from the army. More than 20 of my friends and relatives have been killed by the army." Women who fight against the violence of the development do so at the risk of losing their lives.

Women's Health Threatened by Industrialization

The key to the free market in the Asia-Pacific region is industrialization spurred by foreign investment. Export processing zones are multiplying, with young women acting as the major labor force. One young Indonesian worker testified at the Women's Tribunal about how she organized a strike to protest low wages and "underwear checks" which were required of women asking for menstruation leave. This woman, who was a leader of the strike, was arrested and interrogated.

Two women from Thailand testified about health hazards on the job. One of the two appeared to be in a great deal of pain. Her body was bent over and her lower back was in a cast. She told of how she fell while carrying 50 kilograms of supplies, and was taken to the hospital. A short while later, when her worker's accident compensation insurance expired, she was released from the hospital, though she was still not well. When she testified, she was still suffering the after effects of the injury. In addition to the physical pain, she faces a crisis of survival, since she has a child and her husband was injured in a traffic accident.

The other woman worked in a spinning mill. Her lungs were damaged because of insufficient ventilation, and she had not yet recovered though she quit her job several years earlier. Despite her ill health, she is currently trying to tackle the problem of occupational health. Hearing these voices of suffering coming from underneath the rapid prosperity of Thai economy, the question we asked ourselves again was, "development for whom?"

Searching for an Alternative Society

While gender violence intertwined with structural violence threatens the well-being of women in Asia, women at the grass roots fight back by trying to change their pain into strength. This fight is not only against the immediate violence, but calls into question the economic and social systems, political power structures, and cultural values that produce the violence.

Asian women are preparing enthusiastically for the UN Conference on Women which will be held in Beijing in the Fall of 1995. It will be the first such conference to be held in Asia. At the Mexico Conference of 1975, Asian women were not visible, but they have become active in the intervening decades. They are now very active in a search for an alternative to replace the current development model. They want to create an "Asia of human rights" in the 21st century, rather than an "Asia of development."

In order to fulfill this grand aim, they have proposed the formation of a network of Asian women who are engaged in alternative activities, no matter how small they may be, to share their experiences. Many women in many places are pursuing alternative activities: integrated farming in Thailand, trade of pesticide-free bananas from Negros Island, the Philippines, to Japan; making soap by hand in various locations in Japan; and other alternative activities, which are reported to be ongoing in many rural and urban locals in India.

Accompanying these grassroots activities, a trend of thought is spreading internationally which reevaluates the current development model from the viewpoint of women in the South, connecting ecology and feminism. Vandana Shiva of India is one of its leading proponents. She argues that we need to question the sacredness given to modern scientific technology and economic development. It is not universal, but rather a spiritual product of Western patriarchy. The modern world exists only at the cost of sacrificing nature, women, and the third world. She further criticizes modern society as one in which only market prices matter, and she stresses the role that women must play in the struggle to regain a nature and society in which the survival of all living thing is placed in the center.

We hope that the "Asian 21st century" will become a "women's 21st century," a century where women take the initiative in creating a world in which men and women, people and nature, all ethnic groups, and the "North" and "South" can live in a harmony. This will mean, essentially, creating a new civilization.

5

Ten Years Under the
Equal Employment Opportunity Law

Nakano Mami

The stated aims of the Equal Employment Opportunity Law (EEOL), which went into effect on April 1, 1986, were eliminating sexual discrimination in all forms of employment; promoting equal opportunity and treatment in employment; harmonizing work and family life; and respecting women's maternity.

The law, however, proved to be ineffective, for several reasons:

1) The articles concerning recruitment and hiring, assignment and promotion only require employers to make voluntary "endeavors";
2) There are no punitive measures for violations of the agreements on vocational training, fringe benefits, retirement age, resignations and dismissals;
3) An Equal Opportunity Mediation Committee was established to address sexual discrimination, but it cannot involve itself in any case unless there is agreement between the disputing parties; and
4) In contrast to these insufficient measures, there was a relaxation or outright abandonment of restrictions against women working overtime, on holidays, and late at night.

The EEOL was passed and put into force at roughly the same time as another piece of legislation, the Workers Dispatch Act, which legalized the dispatch of workers as a means to enable smooth adjustments in the labor market based on supply and demand. Moreover, the Labor Standards Law provision concerning working hours was changed to allow "flexible working-hour systems" on a large scale, enabling employers to impose longer than eight-hour shifts without extra overtime payments, in exchange for some small curtailment of weekly working hours.

Backed by these changes, enterprises have promoted the following workforce policies:

1) Treatment of workers purely on the basis of ability and accomplishment. This was fixed in accordance with the EEOL, which called for companies to judge women individually, on the basis of their "abilities and willingness," rather than collectively on the basis of their gender;
2) The development of policies used to segregate workers according to job type (managerial or general clerical) and in terms of employment (full-time or part-time);
3) An attempt to make employment more fluid and working conditions more flexible, backed by the legalization of the workers' dispatch system and the revision allowing for more flexible working hours. This is being done in order to enable managers to adjust personnel placement and working hours in accordance with work volume and economic fluctuations; and
4) The enthusiastic use of female workers to compensate for the lack of young male workers.

In practice, this use of women's labor has turned out to be nothing but a rationalization for and stabilizing mechanism for wage gaps between men and women. Companies operate under the pretext that women, who bear the brunt of family responsibilities, cannot sacrifice their family life as men do. By so doing they confine women primarily to part-time employment where unstable positions and bad working conditions are a given.

Figure 5.1. **Numbers of Part-Time Workers**

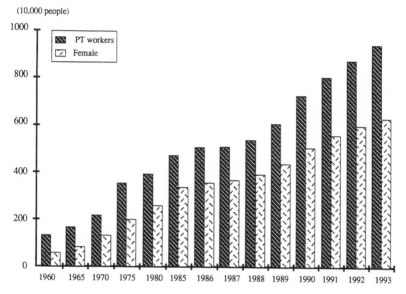

Source: Ministry of Labor.

Greater Female Participation in Labor

Women have been encouraged to enter into the labor market during the past ten years. The number of women in the workforce has been steadily increasing since 1985, the year when the EEOL was enacted. According to the Ministry of Labor's *Labor Force Survey*, the number of working women jumped from 15,480,000 to 20,090,000 between 1985 and 1993. In the same period, women went from making up 35.9% of the total workforce to 38.6% But in fact, this advance is largely due to an increase in the number of female part-time workers. In 1960, just 570,000 people worked fewer than 34 hours a week, but this number swelled to 3,330,000 in 1985 and to 6,230,000 in 1993, accounting for a full 31.8% of the total female workforce. In other words, of the 4.6 million women who entered the workforce between 1985 and 1993, 2.9 million were part-timers (see Figure 5.1).

The number of part-time workers is even larger if we include those who work over 35 hours a week but who are not treated as full-timers. Women tend to accept these limitations because they take it for granted that full-timers must work long hours and cannot maintain a balance between work and family life.

An increasing number of women today are postponing marriage to enter the labor market. As a result, women are marrying later. Young women are reluctant to marry and have children, partially because the work environment does not allow them to strike a balance between work and family responsibilities; working conditions are poor; and social support systems for childbirth and child-rearing are insufficient. This is behind the drop in the birth rate in 1993 to 1.46.

The Effects of the Recession

During the current economic recession, women's participation in the workforce has failed to keep up with the figures for men in both numbers and in ratio. In 1993, women made up 40.5% of the total work force, 0.2 percentage points lower than the figure for the previous year. In addition, there has been little improvement over the past ten years in the so-called M-shape in the female employment curve (see Figure 5.2). The group of those aged 34 to 40 is the least represented at work. This shows that the dominant work pattern for women is to quit their jobs at the time of marriage or childbirth, and to reenter the workforce later. Enterprise restructuring has resulted in personnel cuts and other changes that have had particularly severe effects on women. There has been a conspicuous increase in the number of women being urged to quit upon marriage or childbirth, and in middle-aged and elderly women being urged to retire. Many changes have been instituted with the covert aim of forcing women to quit. Far from considering the establishment of child care and family care leaves, companies have extended working hours and increased transfers to distant places, thus making it virtually impossible for women to continue to work.

Figure 5.2. **Women in Workforce, by Age Group**

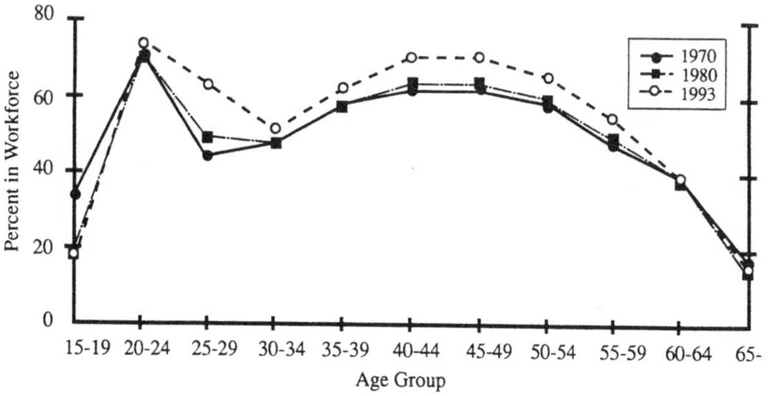

Source: Ministry of Labor.

The difficulty new women graduates are having finding work and the discriminatory treatment they receive indicates the seriousness of the situation facing women. For some time after the enactment of the EEOL, there seemed to be a growing equality between men and women—more new women graduates were getting jobs, and more women were being promoted to important posts. We realize now that at that time companies were simply short-handed due to the so-called "bubble" economy. With the current recession, the employment rate for new women graduates has dropped much lower than it was ten years ago. As of October 1, 1994, only 61.5% of new female graduates had received unofficial offers of employment, in contrast to 78.5% of their male counterparts. Among the complaints voiced by new women graduates were: they were denied the opportunity to get information—they failed to receive responses to their requests for company brochures; they were not allowed to attend some meetings for new graduates; they were not allowed to take some employment examinations; and they were excluded by the imposition of such discriminatory conditions as "we only accept students who live with their parents" and "we only accept unmarried students."

In addition, there have been quite a few complaints concerning sexual harassment. Some interviewers insult new women graduates by intentionally and persistently taking up the subject of looks and physical appearance, and some harass them sexually while hinting at the possibility of employment. These abuses of power by interviewers go beyond the limits of endurance—they make use of their advantageous positions over new women graduates, as they are well aware of the imbalance between supply and demand in the employment market. The ethics of Japanese company men need to be thoroughly questioned. Discrimination at the stages of recruitment and employment is especially inimical, since it occurs at the entrance gate and against people who have no work experience and thus no idea of how to cope with the situation. The fact that discrimination of this kind exists strengthens suspicions of continued discriminatory treatment by companies in placement, promotion, wage, and other areas.

Discrimination in Promotions and Wages

According to *Workforce Research*, 200,000 women held managerial posts in 1993. This seems to indicate progress if compared to the 1985 figure of 140,000. A closer examination reveals, though, that since 1991, the figure has stagnated. According to the 1992 *Basic Investigation of Women in Managerial Posts*, in companies with more than 30 employees women made up just 1.2%, 2.3%, and 6.4%, respectively, of posts equivalent to department head, section head, and subsection head. This promotion gap between men and women has led to a huge gap in wages, which has been repeatedly noted by the International Labor Organization. In 1985, the year that EEOL was enacted, women earned 51.8% of what men made (including part-time workers). In 1990 the figure fell to 49.6%, then rose to 51.8% in 1992. This was still lower, though, than the 52.1% figure in 1986, the year the law was enforced.

There is a general tendency for men's wages to rise steadily

Figure 5.3. **Monthly Wages, Compared by Gender**

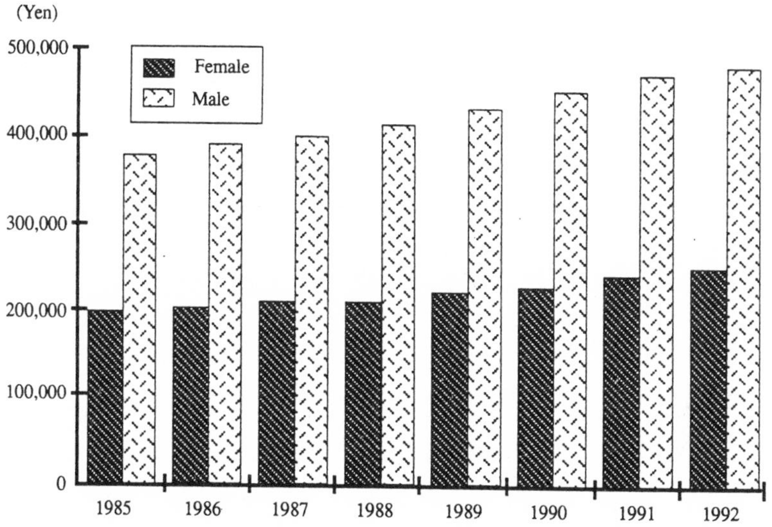

Source: Ministry of Labor.

and reach a peak at around the age of 50 to 54, while for women the wages begin to fall as they enter their thirties (see Figure 5.3). Hence the longer they work, the greater the wage gap. The wage gap shown in fixed salaries for women and men (excluding part-time workers) is 91.5 to 100 for the group aged 18 to 24, and 51.2 to 100 for the group aged 50 to 54. The main factors contributing to the wage gap are as follows:

1) The sexual division of labor remains, and women's work is still considered a means "to help support the household economy." Thus women's basic salaries are often lower than those of men, and women are often excluded from allowances paid to "heads of households";
2) Women still face deep-rooted discriminatory treatment in placement, promotion, and vocational training; and
3) Segregation has been promoted with the diversification of job

types and terms of employment, etc., which were widely introduced after the EEOL was enforced.

The Dual-Track Employment System

Companies introduced a dual-career track employment system when the EEOL was enforced. The aim of this system was to divide workers into two groups—managerial and general clerical—at the time of employment. The workers' future treatment would be decided according to which group she or he was assigned to. This system soon proved to be a mere pretext for stabilizing and even expanding the existing sexual discrimination against women, since women were placed into the subsidiary group at the starting gate, or were excluded from the managerial group because of the imposition of transfers to faraway places and long working hours. The companies knew it would be virtually impossible for most women to accept these conditions. In the companies where this system was introduced, the wage gap between men and women begins with the starting salary, the excuse being the "difference in the type of work"—difference in track or group, even when there is little difference between the two groups in terms of work content.

Companies have allowed some token women to enter the managerial track, under the condition that they devote themselves to the company as thoroughly as do their male counterparts. The number of women in managerial tracks is still very small. In addition to this forced devotion, these women workers are often deprived of opportunities to exert their abilities, hindered by walls of deep-rooted sexual discrimination, and obliged to be content with slower promotion even when they exercise their abilities.

Balancing Private and Professional Life

Because women generally work for a short period, companies hesitate to invest in training them to be executives or to pay them reasonable wages. Companies do not deem investments in women to be effective. They exclude women from recruitment and employment, job rotations and promotions, and education and training. Nevertheless, given the tendency for more and more women to return to work after child-bearing or child-rearing, it seems clear that they have a strong desire to work. The average period women spend working has steadily increased and rose above the seven-year mark in 1990.

Still today, many women resign their jobs in order to marry, have and/or rear children. This is because companies suggest that they do so, or because difficult working conditions make it difficult for them to continue work after child-bearing. The division of roles by gender remains. For example, according to "Monthly Statistics on Labor," men worked an average of 2,038.8 per year in 1993, compared to just 1,734 for women. The January 1994 report on "Overwork and Its Effects on Health," issued by the Economic Planning Agency, says that men worked an average of 2,508 hours per year, and that one in six worked over 3,100 hours, which is considered to be within the danger zone for "*karoshi*" or death from overwork.

In contrast, women put in a much lower figure of 2,002 hours, 500 hours fewer than that of men. Still, the figure is higher than those of other countries. The policy of decreasing working hours has affected women differently from men, but according to a survey conducted by the Women's Bureau of Rengo (the Japanese Trade Unions Confederation), working women slept only an average of 6.50 hours a night, compared with more than seven hours for men. Women are generally responsible for housework and find themselves with much less free time.

Needless to say, the situation for women on the managerial track, who are required to work as hard as men, is more severe. With the implementation of the EEOL, restrictions on overtime work, such as work on holidays and after midnight, were drastically relaxed or removed. For example, the restriction on overtime work to two hours a day was abolished. Currently, holiday work is allowed one day in every four weeks in nonindustrial fields. Women would have great difficulty working the tremendous number of hours that men put in. In addition, many women in management positions are sent to work in other cities, meaning that they must leave their families behind. Living apart causes serious problems for couples in terms of marriage, child-bearing and child-rearing.

The tendency for women to retire early has also been pointed out. This is because companies lack understanding and concern for employees' family life when rotating personnel. Some companies are already saying that "the era of women in the managerial track is over."

With the implementation of the EEOL and women's entry into the workforce, death from overwork, which was traditionally a "men's issue," has become something for women to be concerned about as well. One 22-year-old women working for Fuji Bank died of an asthma attack, and it was reported that she had been working until midnight on a daily basis. Her parents believe that the bank was responsible for her death because it forced her to work extremely long hours. They sued the company, demanding compensation. A ruling was not issued in this well-publicized case, however, since it was settled out of court.

Targets of Workforce Discrimination

There is no doubt that women's inclusion in the work force has been promoted since the implementation of the EEOL. Women now do jobs which were dominated by men a decade or so ago even in companies where women's jobs were originally differentiated from men's jobs. Now, however, these jobs are being done by part-time workers. Some high-skill jobs which were originally done by people on the managerial track, and thus led to key positions, have been downgraded to the assistant track. Jobs that were once done by people on the assistant track are now being transferred to part-time workers. The women doing these jobs are being paid far less than men were ten years ago. Although women are required to do high-level jobs and to make decisions, they are still called "assistants," or low status part-time workers. One of the features of the post EEOL labor situation is that women have been included in the main workforce, but still face discrimination.

Companies now need only a small number of men to be their regular employees, and these elite workers are expected to reach the top of the corporate pyramid. Companies have come to believe that other employees do not need to be regular employees. They are not expected to work until retirement age and have to work under discriminatory labor conditions symbolized by job instability and low wages.

The situation of part-time airline flight attendants offers a good example of this. Japan Air Lines recently announced that it had decided to begin hiring part-time flight attendants dispatched from other companies on three-year contracts, paying them ¥1,000 per hour. When the Ministry of Transport objected to this practice, companies responded by conducting a mass media campaign with slogans such as "What's the matter with part-time workers?" and "That's rude to part-time workers." This diverted attention from the essential issue. As a result, the Ministry of Transport gave in and Japan Air Lines has hired part-time flight attendants, with the provision that the company give them the opportunity to become regular employees.

Along with the liberalization of trade and deregulation, "an excessive drop in prices" is already under way. An extreme "decline in wages" is also expected to occur with the increased participation of women in the workforce and discrimination against women. It is extremely important for Japanese corporations to promote such policies because they need to strengthen their competitiveness vis-à-vis their Asian counterparts. There is a job shortage for female students in terms of regular employment. However, if women are willing to develop their abilities as part-time workers and to receive low wages, there is no such shortage. The "Don't expect too much" campaign by companies targeting women has already begun in the mass media.

Strengthening the Corporate Society

"Corporate society" is, in a word, a society whose structure is male-centered. Men can put their lives in the companies' hands. The "Three Sacred Treasures" of the Japanese employment system, including lifetime employment and the seniority system, strengthen workers' subordination to their companies. Furthermore, the "merit system," which has been strengthened since the implementation of the EEOL, has brought about a comprehensive obedience and "selfless devotion" to companies. The "merit system," where wages and promotions depend on an evaluation of ability, is not based upon objective evaluations such as skills, experiences and types of businesses the worker is engaged in. It is based upon the workers' willingness or ability to devote or sacrifice themselves to their companies by working overtime or working in other cities and leaving their families behind. Such evaluation methods leave room for bias based on the assessors' or bosses' prejudices. Workers who receive a poor evaluation cannot expect promotions and will not earn enough money to support their families. Therefore, their personal values and private lives become restricted. The assessment includes the worker's "performance," which should be a relatively objective factor, but "performance" competition between workers leads them to do unlimited amounts of work as they aim for promotion.

Labor unions ought to have a role to play in mitigating this promotion of workers' subordination to the companies, and in preventing competition between workers, but the unions' activities within corporations are rather limited. If a company loses its competitive edge in the market, it cannot survive, and this would mean that workers in the firm would lose their jobs. Therefore it is, in a way, natural for this thinking to prevail among company unions. We cannot expect such unions to express opinions or take actions which might endanger their companies' survival.

It is thus understandable that women, whose lives are seen as based upon the concerns of daily life, are excluded from the structure of corporate society. The EEOL, as mentioned before, aims to guarantee equal opportunities for women based upon their "capabilities and willingness." In this way, the law has strengthened the above-mentioned atmosphere of outright competition. The simultaneous progress of women's participation in the workforce and discrimination against women, which seem to be contradictory, is the by-product of the corporate-society structure and the EEOL. It is important to note that, as a result of such policies and the recent economic recession, the employment of salaried men has also been threatened. In order to strengthen their chance for survival, companies will continue to promote these policies.

Prospects for Equality

It is extremely important that women acquire a status equal to that of men. We must influence the economic world in order to transform corporate society into a type of society where nature and the lives of human beings are respected. Equality should mean that men participate in family life and exercise their right to participate in child-rearing. This could provide men with an escape from selfless devotion to companies and restore their humanity. In Japanese corporate society, private life is horribly neglected, both in terms of how countries operate and how workers, who shoulder the industrial economy, are treated. As a result, women are discriminated against in terms of wages, while men are discriminated against in terms of the right to participate in family life.

The question of "equality or protection," and the provision of protection for women alone, has been one of the big issues of contention in the struggle for equal employment for women and men. Men's working conditions are far below international standards set by ILO conventions, while the conditions for women manage to meet the international standards. The gap between women and men in terms of working conditions should be eliminated through the improvement of men's working conditions. They should be the same as women's. It is understandable that the Council on the Issues of Women and Children has recommended the institution of a working environment which would eliminate gender roles and enable both women and men to carry responsibilities both in the workplace and at home.

The problems of a company-centered society, such as long working hours (epitomized by death from overwork) and work in distant cities away from the family, have been criticized globally, because such problems affect workers' health, family life and their children's education. In some cases, companies have come to recognize that a company-centered society does not necessarily contribute to the effective use of personnel. The government has also pointed out the necessity of transforming the "corporate-centered society" into a "cooperative society of women and men," or a society in which private life is respected. As a result of workers' demands, childcare leave and nursing care leave have been established, and we can see that the government is heading toward the ratification of the ILO 156 Convention. However, in order to transform the structure of society toward equality between women and men, traditional policies related to corporations must be changed drastically. An urgent task for the government is to implement laws to enable the balancing of family and professional life. The following steps are necessary: (1) a reexamination of the tax system in which a household is considered one unit and the income of women considered just a supplement to the family budget; (2) establishing equal rights for workers in various forms of employment; (3) a radical reexamination of the EEOL to ensure de facto equality in recruitment and treatment within companies; (4) enforcing without exceptions the regulations on working hours for both women and men; and (5) limiting transfers to cities far away from families.

Appendix: Excerpts from the Equal Employment Opportunity Law

Chapter I. General provisions

Purpose

1. The purpose of this Law is to promote equal opportunity and treatment between men and women in employment in accordance with the principle contained in the Constitution of Japan ensuring equality under the law; foster measures for women workers, including the development and improvement of their vocational abilities, the provision of assistance for their re-employment, and attempts to harmonize their working life with family life; and thereby to further the welfare and improve this status of women workers.

Basic aspects

2. In view of the fact that women workers contribute to the development of the economy and society and at the same time have a significant role to play as a member of the family in nursing children—who will be the mainstay of the future—the basic objectives of the improvement of the welfare of women workers as outlined in this Law are to enable them to obtain job satisfaction by making effective use of their abilities, with due respect for their maternity but without discriminatory treatment on the basis of sex, and to achieve harmony between their working life and family life.

3. Women workers shall, in awareness that they are members of the working community, endeavor, by their own initiative, to develop, improve and make good use of their abilities in their working life.

Responsibilities of the persons concerned

4. Employers, the State and local public bodies shall endeavor to promote the welfare of women workers according to the basic aspects outlined in sections 2 and 3.

5. The state and local public bodies shall conduct the necessary educational campaigns to increase public interest and understanding in regard to the welfare of women workers, to promote the awareness of women workers that they are members of working community, and especially to remove the factors preventing women workers from making effective use of their abilities.

Chapter II. Promotion of equal opportunity and treatment between men and women in employment

Part 1. Measures to be taken by employers, etc.

6. With regard to the recruitment and hiring of workers, employers shall endeavor to give women opportunity equal to that of men.

7. With regard to the assignment and promotion of workers, employers shall endeavor to treat women workers and men workers equally.

8. With regard to the vocational training for the acquisition of basic skills necessary for workers to perform their duties as provided by ordinance of the Ministry of Labour, employers shall not discriminate against a woman worker as compared with a man by reason of her being a woman.

9. With regard to loans for housing and other similar fringe benefits as provided by ordinance of the Ministry of Labour, employers shall not discriminate against a woman worker as compared with a man by reason of her being a woman.

10. (1) With regard to the compulsory retirement age and dismissal of workers, employers shall not discriminate against a woman worker as compared with a man by reason of her being a woman.

(2) Employers shall not stipulate marriage, pregnancy or childbirth as a reason for resignation of women workers.

(3) Employers shall not dismiss a woman worker by reason of marriage, pregnancy or childbirth or for taking the leave stipulated in section 65, subsection (1) or (2), of the Labor Standard Law.

6

Policies of the Japanese Government Toward Women

Hayashi Yoko

It has been ten years since the ratification, in 1985, of the UN Convention on Elimination of All Forms of Discrimination Against Women (CEDAW).

The Japanese government was initially hesitant to ratify the Convention after it was adopted at the UN General Assembly in 1979. But at the 1980 Copenhagen Conference (during the UN Decade for Women) it signed it, and just before the Nairobi Conference (the last year of the UN Decade for Women) it finally ratified it.

This was achieved through the efforts of women's groups all over Japan, by the work of female Diet members and by women in the mass media who shaped public opinion.

The CEDAW obligates signatories not only to abolish discriminatory laws against women, but also to take measures to abolish discriminatory customs. It is said that the Convention aims not only at "equality before the law" (*de jure* equality) but also "substantial equality" (*de facto* equality).

This article surveys how the Japanese government has dealt with the problem of "gender equality" in bringing "legal" and "substantial" reforms in the past ten years.

Equality in Employment

The central reason for the Japanese government's hesitation to ratify the CEDAW was that Japan did not have the legal framework required by the Convention to prohibit discrimination against women in employment.[1] Just before ratifying it, however, the government enacted the Equal Employment Opportunity Law (EEOL), claiming that this fully provided the required standards. Suspicions remain, however, that the EEOL violates the Convention.

What is clear, in any case, is that this law has not changed the workplace for Japanese women over the past decade.[2] At present, women make up 38% of the total workforce, and their average length of service has increased to 7.3 years. Their salaries, however, are only 60.2% (and this excludes part-timers) of what men earn. If we include part-time workers this rate drops to just 49%.

Many companies reacted to the enactment of the EEOL by introducing a "career-track system" for their employees. They divided their employees into two categories; managerial track, or *sogo shoku,* and general clerical work, or *ippan shoku.* People in the *ippan shoku* track are never transferred to other branches, and this is where women have found themselves. Companies manage women and men differently. There have been many reported cases of women choosing *sogo shoku* to work the same amount as men but facing discrimination in placement and promotion, and being forced into conditions where they cannot cooperate with the other women in *ippan shoku.*

The government, for its part, began a policy to cope with the "problem" of decreasing children.[3] The Day Care Leave Act was enacted in 1992, and workers, regardless of sex, in both public and private sectors can take a leave for one year to take care of infants. Starting in April 1994, 25% of the salary has been provided to employees during their leave, and they have been exempted from local taxes. A similar act to allow workers to take leaves to take care of aging parents has been introduced in the Diet and will soon be passed.

We can thus see that the government is trying to encourage

women to work longer, while at the same time allowing them to have children and giving them time to take care of them. During the last decade, however, there have been no new policy initiatives to give equal treatment to women in employment.

The reason the Japanese government can ignore demands by women for equal treatment is that it does not recognize them as individual human beings, who are expected to work under certain conditions to support their lives. The government sees all women as "housewives," or workers giving partial support to their families. The tax and social insurance systems treat married women as possessions of their husbands, labeling them "dependent family members," and encourages them to work only enough to receive an income which is not high enough to be taxable.

The demands of the women's labor movement are equal payment and the establishment of affirmative action programs. They are calling for a substantial revision of the EEOL, which merely says that "employers have the duty to achieve" goals in promotion, recruitment, and employment. Many women also want to see the formulation of a clear definition of sexual harassment as well as the establishment of provisions to punish assailants.

Along with these movements, women are questioning the tax system, which contains preferential treatment for "housewives," and hope that the system will change to make the unit the "individual" rather than the "household."

Equality under the Family Law

It came as a blow to many women when the government failed to revise the family law at the time it ratified the CEDAW. The government insisted that the Civil Code guarantees "equal rights for women and men" and that there was no need to revise it before ratifying the Convention.

During the past decade, however, many cases have been filed demanding, for instance, that married couples be able to bear different surnames, the abolition of discrimination against children born out of wedlock, or the abolition of a provision which forces women to wait six months after a divorce before remarrying. In a case involving discrimination against children born out of wedlock in terms of inheritance, the Tokyo High Court ruled in 1993 that this practice was unconstitutional, and the Supreme Court is now set to issue its own ruling.

In the midst of this, the Ministry of Justice began a revision of the Family Law in 1991 and issued a "draft for a platform for revising the Civil Code" in July 1994. At present, a council is collecting opinions from experts in various fields. Concrete plans for the revision have not yet been made, so I will point out the critiques that women have of the current Civil Code:

(1) Marriageable age

The Civil Code stipulates that men must be at least 18, and women at least 16, to be able to marry. This treatment, however, is discriminatory and should be changed.

(2) Period of prohibited remarriage

In a very discriminatory provision, women are prohibited from remarrying until six months after a divorce. It is explained that the goal of this provision is to avoid confusion over the identity of the father in case the woman becomes pregnant. However, at present it is possible to identify the father of a baby through medical examination.

(3) Denial of legitimacy by mother

Babies who are born to a married woman are automatically presumed to be the husband's, but the husband has the right to deny patrimony. This provision can deprive mothers, children, and real fathers the right to know the truth. The law should be revised to give mothers a say in regard to the granting of legitimacy.

(4) Forcing married couples to bear the same surname

Under the Civil Code, married couples must bear the same surname, and in 97% of cases couples use the husband's name. This provision discriminates against women who want to retain their own family names. The freedom to choose one's own family name should be guaranteed.

(5) Discrimination against children born out of wedlock[4]

Under the Civil Code, an illegitimate child receives only half the inheritance amount given to a legitimate child. The rationale behind this provision is that it protects legitimate marriage. This should not, however, be used as a reason for discrimination against their children. We must abolish this discrimination. Until recently, legitimate children have been listed as "first son" or "first daughter" in residential cards and family registers, whereas children born out of wedlock were listed simply as "child." In 1994, however, the Ministry of Home Affairs issued a circular notice saying that all children should be listed simply as "child." The Supreme Court will soon issue a ruling concerning the discriminatory provision concerning inheritance, and there is strong possibility it will be deemed unconstitutional.

In addition to the above, some part of the draft of the Civil Code revision written by the Ministry of Justice suggests the introduction of "no-fault divorces."[5] Some women are criticizing this.

Reproductive Health and Rights

The Criminal Code, which was drafted in 1908, prohibited abortion, and the government encouraged a "more births, more children" policy during World War II. After Japan's defeat this policy was changed into one of population control, and the Eugenic Protection Act legalized abortion in some cases.

This Eugenic Protection Act derives from the National Eugenic Act which was devised by the Nazis. It aims at the annihilation of inferior genes by means of abortion. Under this law, "economic reason" can be sufficient grounds for abortion, as can pregnancy caused by rape and threats to the mother's health. It is possible to say that Japanese women acquired the "right to abortion" earlier than women in other countries, but punishments for abortion remain in the Criminal Code.[6] Proposals to eliminate the economic reason from the provisions of the Eugenic Protection Act were submitted to the Diet in 1972, 1973, 1982, and 1983, but they did not pass.

The law does not stipulate how late into the pregnancy an abortion can be performed. In a 1989 ordinance by the Vice Minister in the Ministry of Welfare, the period was cut from 24 weeks to 22 weeks. It can be said that this action demonstrates the government's fears of a falling birth rate.

In addition, the Eugenic Protection Act requires the "consent" of the unborn child's father before allowing an abortion to be performed. This violates the women's right to an abortion as one of the rights of privacy.

There are many other problems concerning reproductive health and rights. One major issue today is the rapid development of reproductive technology. No brakes have yet been placed on the commercial use of surrogate mothers or surrogate deliveries. Last year 13,000 people used in-vitro fertilization, but the use of fertilized embryos is not under the control of any law. The government depends on moral regulation by the Medical Association for decisions on the use of fertilized embryos. The long- and short-term effects of the use of hormones on women's bodies must be more carefully studied and publicized.

Political Participation

In 1946, when the first election was held in which women could participate, 39 women were elected to the House of Representatives. The following year, however, their number dropped to 15 and has not recovered since. In the House of Councilors 12 women were elected in 1950, since then their numbers have gradually increased and in 1989 came to a peak with 33 elected women. It is said that it is easier for women to win seats in the House of Councilors, which has a proportional district system, compared to the House of Representatives, which has typically

Table 6.1

Number of Diet Members, by Gender

	Diet Members			Lower House			Upper House		
	Total	Female	%	Total	Female	%	Total	Female	%
1975	726	25	3.4	475	7	1.5	251	18	7.2
1980	762	26	3.4	511	9	1.8	251	17	6.8
1985	752	27	3.6	504	8	1.6	248	19	7.7
1990	762	46	6.0	510	12	2.4	252	34	14.7
1993	762	52	6.8	511	14	2.7	251	38	15.1

Source: National Diet Secretariats.

Table 6.2

Number of Prefectural Governors, City Mayors, and Heads of Towns and Villages, by Gender

	Prefectural Governors		City Mayors		Heads of Towns and Villages	
	Female	Male	Female	Male	Female	Male
1980	0	47	0	644	2	2
1985	0	47	0	650	2	2
1990	0	47	0	660	1	2

Source: National Diet Secretariats.

had multimember districts. In the 1989 House of Councilors election, Doi Takako, the chairperson of the Social Democratic Party of Japan (SDPJ), helped many women to be elected amidst a voter upswell against the consumption tax.

We need to review the electoral system today and to get political parties to formulate affirmative action policies to allow women to participate in the process of decision-making.

Today the political arena is in the midst of the largest reform since World War II. A new electoral law, based on single-member districts, has been enacted. No election has been held under the new system yet, but many people predict that the number of women members of the Diet will fall even further due to harsh competition and political parties' ignorance toward encouraging women candidates.

In addition, the SDPJ, which once stood women candidates under a platform of "protecting the Constitution" and "peace," changed its basic policy as it formed a coalition with the Liberal Democratic Party (LDP). It is uncertain where the few million or so women who once voted for the SDPJ will go. Many people now feel that it is critical for Japanese women to create a new political movement centering on grassroots/feminist movements, which will replace the SDPJ. My view is that the conditions for Japanese women in the future will be greatly affected by the outcome of such efforts.

Notes

1. The 1947 Labor Standards Law required employers to pay equal wages to men and women for equal work and set penalties for violations of this principle, but this only applied to wages, and no laws existed to prevent discrimination in nonwage areas. For this reason, discrimination in, for instance, mandatory retirement ages, was long the subject of court struggles.

2. Please see chapter 5 for more details.

3. In 1989, Japan's birthrate (the number of children an average woman bears during her lifetime) dropped to 1.57, the lowest or second-lowest in the world. A phrase "1.57 shock," was even coined as a result.

4. In 1947, 3.79% of Japanese children were born out of wedlock, but by 1988 this had dropped to just 1.01%, a figure lower even than the prewar period. If we compare this to figures for Europe, which run between 20 and 50%, we can get an idea of the strength of social support for the institution of marriage and the depth of prejudice and discrimination against unwed mothers.

5. Under amendments proposed by the Ministry of Justice, the divorce system would be changed from the previous policy—that people entering a marriage do not have the right to dissolve it—to one in which divorces would be granted when a marriage was judged to be bankrupt, for instance if the couple lived apart for a certain period of time.

6. Articles 212–216 of the Criminal Code define the "crime of abortion" and set a penalty of up to one year's imprisonment for women violating the statute.

7

Military Slavery and the
Women's Movement

Yamazaki Hiromi

It was only in the 1990s that Japanese women began a full-scale commitment to the so-called "comfort women" issues. The words "comfort women" have long been known, but until recently, no in-depth research has been undertaken, nor have the issues ever been tackled in terms of what it means to women and to the Japanese. The Japanese women's movement should be criticized and held accountable for neglecting the issues and the victims for as long as 50 years.

In the sense that the Japanese government has not really apologized or offered compensation for the victims, the women's movement has fallen short of fulfilling its task. Meanwhile new commitments have imposed a substantial challenge on the women's movement, a challenge largely inspired by a new definition of the case. UN-related sources came to define the "comfort women" program through a series of new facts, as sexual slavery by the Japanese military in the form of systematic state sexual violence. The introduction of a precise terminology, i.e., sexual slavery, appears to have greatly inspired an all-out commitment by Japanese women, who had long been unsatisfied with the original term: *"jugun ianfu*" (*jugun* = accompanying the military, *ianfu* = a woman who brings rest and comfort). The new definition signifies that what is in question is a fundamental relationship between the state, sexuality, and war. Although this article uses the older words "comfort women" to refer to those historical facts, what it is meant to signify is something close to the new definition; i.e., military sexual slavery by Japan.

What Was Japanese Military Sexual Slavery?

An extensive deployment of "comfort stations" for the exclusive use of the military started in December 1937, concurrent with the Nanking massacre. However the first establishment—according to a government study—dates back to 1932 in Shanghai.

The main impetus in setting up "comfort stations" was the prevalence of not only massacre and plunder, but rape by the Japanese army during its operations in Shanghai and Nanjing. However, the objective was not to eliminate rape itself. Military sexual slavery was employed out of crucial need to control the outburst of Japanese soldiers' sexual drive. V.D. checkups served to maintain the health and hygiene of the battling army. It was thought that providing an outlet for sexual desires through the use of "comfort stations" would alleviate soldiers' frustrations and help to decrease complaints against the military. The employment of Korean and local women, who did not know Japanese, helped to prevent military secrets from leaking out. Although the military code stipulated strict punishments for rape because it would aggravate the anti-Japanese sentiment of local residents, few reports were actually filed, as offenders' superiors were also supposed to be punished.

So far, evidence of "comfort stations" has been confirmed in China, Hong Kong, the Philippines, Malaysia, Singapore, British-colonized Borneo, Indonesia, Thailand, Burma, New Guinea, and Okinawa. It is believed, however, that "comfort stations" were set up almost everywhere Japanese troops were stationed, including the southwest Pacific islands and Japan. Victimized women other than the Japanese women (who will be referred to later in this chapter), were first women from the Japanese colonies in Taiwan, Korea, and then China, and later, women from countries occupied by Japan. Dutch captives were also victimized in Indonesia. In the case of Korean women, most of them were lied to and were led to believe they would be working as nurses, or in a factory; some were just taken by force. In occupied Philippines many of the victims were raped first and then brought to "comfort stations." The ages varied from 11 or 12 years old to the late 20s.

Styles of "comfort stations" differed. Some were run directly by the military, some were managed by civil agents under military control, others were private brothels temporarily held by the military. Women were also dragged over to the front line and forced to serve sexually, or were confined by individual or multiple soldiers personally. In all cases, women were locked inside a room, given meager food, exposed daily to physical abuse and raped by dozens of soldiers every day—a condition which can't be called anything other than sexual enslavement.

The degree of involvement of the Japanese government and military differed according to the type of "comfort station." However, at the very least they confirmed and controlled the selection of agents; the recruitment of women; the involvement of military police, civilian police, and consulate in terms of transportation; the provision of logistics (probably funding as well) for agents; transportation of agents and women by the military; the setting of rules, charges, fees, and time for the use of "comfort stations"; the construction of comfort stations; regular V.D. checkups; the distribution of condoms; management, supervision, and control by adjacent troops, accounting officers, and soldiers on day duty (*jugun ianfu shiryoshu*), besides the general planning and formatting of "comfort stations." Military sexual slavery therefore should be considered nothing but a system of sexual violence against women by the state of Japan: a sexual enslavement system whose supreme responsibility resided in the late emperor Showa.

Why Did This Happen?

One of the crucial contributing factors would be a licensed prostitution system. Japan had had a well-organized system of state-licensed prostitution, and the military greatly benefited from this in setting up its own prostitution system. It was quite easy for the military to set up and run "comfort stations" as it was manageable simply by providing assistance to private agencies, who already had thorough knowledge of how to run a brothel.

Victims of the licensed prostitution system were sold by their destitute patriarchs (fathers). The agents drove women out to "comfort stations" in the battlefield by cunningly increasing their debts or by re-selling them to an agent who ran "comfort stations." Although Japanese women were ranked higher and treated better than Korean and local women, they were still victims of sexual enslavement as they were confined and deprived of sexual liberty.

Once Japan's military enslavement system is understood as another version of licensed prostitution, we can understand why Japanese soldiers would have used "comfort stations" without hesitation. They merely continued the act of buying women which they did during peacetime. What was different was that in the battlefield, the enemy woman was considered as a "reward" bestowed by the emperor.

The conceptual underpinnings of buying women and committing rape are what can be called the "phallic myth," which defines male lust as uncontrollable, and its negative twin, the "maternal myth." Under the system of imperial militarism, Japanese women were reduced to reproductive machinery. During the war, their role was to send husbands and sons out to the battlefield and to keep the family safe back home. At the same time, women who served male lust, "prostitutes" and "comfort women," were relegated to the bottom of the hierarchy. Japanese women were separated from women in colonized and occupied territories once they were obliged to bear and raise "emperor's children." This is the backdrop against which Japan's military sexual slavery can be seen as a form of racist violence. This ideological structure neither arose suddenly during the war nor vanished immediately after the war. Even though licensed prostitution was abolished after the war, a policy that authorized prostitution has been kept alive and reproduced in various ways. Women from other Asian countries are being "sexually enslaved" in Japan's sex industry. For the Japanese, overcoming the historical mistake of military sexual slavery has proven to be as difficult as overcoming the phallic and maternal myths.

Survivor Kim Hak Sun

In August 1991, for the first time in South Korea, a former "comfort woman," Kim Hak Sun, openly revealed her past so that she could condemn the Japanese government publicly.

There had been other Korean women who spoke out in Okinawa (Japan) and in Thailand. But Japanese society failed to take the opportunity to re-examine and verify its own history. Kawada Fumiko, who interviewed Pae Pong Gi in Okinawa, recollects that in 1977 when Pae Pong Gi spoke out, lawyers refused to consider filing a compensation claim against the Japanese government.

By the time Kim Hak Sun had spoken out, the situation had greatly changed, largely due to the Korean women's progressive movement. In 1990 Korean women's organizations issued a joint request to the Japanese government to conduct a study on "comfort women" issues and demanded an apology and compensation. It is well known that the Japanese government issued a false statement in the National Diet, ascribing responsibility to private agents, a denial which only served to fuel the protest movement in Korea.

Yun Chung Ok of the Korean Council on the Matter of Comfort Women said: "We must locate those who live abroad, refusing to come home out of shame that they will be physically humiliated, and we must help them live with confidence for the rest of their lives. In order to accomplish this, we need to completely change the social conceptions of women's sexuality" (*Chosen Jin Josei ga Mita Ianfu Mondai*).

In 1985, a women's movement declaration from Korea related the problem of sexual double standards to the "overthrow of patriarchy." Clearly, it is the existence of such a women's movement that finally pulled the "comfort women" issue—which had either been taboo in Korea or was allowed to be seen only through nationalistic perspectives—into the sociopolitical agenda.

Victims who have spoken out have been forced to undergo various public humiliations such as being labeled "dirty," "unworthy of marriage," or "barren." They have also suffered from their own ingrained values toward virginity. So long as this kind of perception is left uncorrected, the victims will continue to be victimized.

It was not a coincidence that testimony by Kim Hak Sun was followed by that of a series of other survivors, and that voices of condemnation from victimized countries such as the Philippines grew increasingly louder against individual perpetrators as well as against the state of Japan and its history of rape and sexual violence. These reactions were a natural consequence of a shift in perceptions in the women's movement as they learned to accept the victims not with pity but with a new understanding that they are survivors who are courageously demanding a solution to this problem.

The Women's Movement in Japan

Starting in the late 1980s, the women's movement in Japan began to problematize the issues of prostitution of Asian women, trafficking in women, mail order brides, rape, sexual harassment, commercialization of sexuality, etc. In the process of doing so, they came to the awareness that marriage and prostitution have played a dual role in sustaining patriarchal society. Men sustain the structure of economic growth as corporate warriors and in order to alleviate stress, it is clear what they do at home and in the sex industry.

At the same time, women from Asia, Thailand, and the Philippines, for instance, came to replace Japanese women at the bottom of the social ladder as prostitutes or housewives. Japanese women could reflect on their position through them as well. Having a common recognition of "patriarchy," Japanese women have started seeking solidarity with other Asian women. At the same time, however, the history of "comfort women" has been left as one obstacle that could not be resolved. While women did tackle Japan's postwar compensation issues, the actual role that women played in the "negative history" hardly entered their consciousness at all. It was not until the Korean women's movement brought to the surface the "comfort women" issue that Japanese women were made to realize and admit to the fact that they were aggressors, and also to recognize that it is their responsibility to face up to this fact and work with the survivors. Finally, we realized that Japanese women stand both as daughters of aggressors and as sisters of victims.

From my experience, this was made possible mainly through Korean women's double perspective on the issue, i.e., racism and sexism. It might sound abstract but they made me realize a consistent pattern of evasion by the Japanese women's postwar movement of the history of colonization and invasion, which in turn sustained the imposition of assimilation on Korean women in Japan as well as the discrimination against them.

Together with Korean women, I am supporting a lawsuit filed by Song Siin Do, a former Korean "comfort woman" resident in Japan, and by doing so, my feelings of responsibility have been strengthened. For almost fifty years, Song has been surrounded by the Japanese aggressors, feeling insecure about whether she would be allowed to stay, and has always felt pressure to offer justification for why she is in Japan. Many Korean women in Japan might recognize a part of themselves in her precarious condition.

While military sexual slavery has been viewed mainly as an international problem, it is necessary to grasp it as a systemic, deep-rooted problem in Japanese society.

We must also confess that Japanese women have almost completely failed to cover the cases of Japanese "comfort women." Although they were citizens of an aggressor nation, they were also, as I mentioned above, themselves victims of a sexual slavery system. We must note the fact that, except for a handful of testimonies made anonymously, they have remained completely silent. That they were "prostitutes" before they went to the battlefields is not the problem. What has forced their silence is Japanese society, which has maintained until today the unconscious reliance on the ruling structure that keeps marriage and prostitution compatible, installs prostitution as a "necessary evil," and thus further discriminates against "prostitutes."

What Strategy Should We Follow?

At present, five lawsuits have been filed by victims of military sexual slavery. Koreans, Filipinas, a Korean resident in Japan, and a Dutch woman are demanding an apology and compensation. A major legal obstacle standing in the way of these lawsuits is the prewar state reparation code, which stipulates state immunity. The Japanese government was absolved of responsibilities for acts of tort. The state of Japan unilaterally declared that it would not bear responsibility for the crimes of its colonial rule and aggressive war.

However, it is a logic unacceptable within international law. Song Siin Do's case points out that Japan's military sexual slavery obviously breached conventions on forced labor, slavery and trafficking in women, and that it also constitutes crimes against humanity. The Japanese government must punish those who were responsible for the perpetration of these crimes. The issue will never be solved unless the state of Japan apologizes and compensates the victims.

From the same point of view, the Korean Council on the Matter of Comfort Women is demanding that the Japanese government comply with the ruling of a Permanent Court of Arbitration which could be established according to international law.

At the time of filing in 1993, Song Siin Do claimed only official apology. It was just recently (January 28, 1995) that her damage was calculated in monetary terms as a supplement to the complaint. Items of damage range from sexual damage, physical damage, deprivation of national identity, and various sequelae, totalling about ¥80 billion. Since this figure is unrealistic for a Japanese court, it was set at ¥120 million, so that it would not fall below the sum paid by the government to war criminals such as Tojo Hideki, and to their wives as military/bereaved families pensions. This demand is also a challenge to public opinion to recognize the gravity of damage caused by military sexual slavery, and to change their historical view.

However, the Japanese government has taken no measures at all on behalf of the victims. While the government's second research report of 1993 partly admitted the responsibilities of the Japanese military, it did not clarify the total number of victims and the persons responsible for the program. The government stated that this is a case that "seriously stained the honor and dignity of many women under the military involvement" and that it would consider ways to demonstrate "feelings of apologies and remorse." A year and a half later, at the end of 1994, the conclusion was presented only to reiterate the old position, saying that compensation "has been dealt with in good faith with the Treaty of Peace with Japan of 1951 (San Francisco Peace Treaty) and other international agreements."

What the government came up with under the rubric of a "future-oriented policy" was the "Peace, Friendship and Exchange Initiative," which promotes exchange with students from abroad while having no relevance to war victims, and the "Asian Peace and Friendship Fund for Women."

The "Asian Peace and Friendship Fund for Women," which is composed of two projects, is a product of the government's refusal to grant individual compensation. As a way to facilitate the "wide participation of the people" (Prime Minister Murayama Tomiichi's statement), that is to say, to erase state responsibility, one project is a "private fund" project for which the government bears only secretariat and advertisement expenses and disburses donations from the private sector to former "comfort women." The other is a project to allocate ODA (official development assistance) to women's NGOs. During the negotiation, the government circulated a secret document confirming that the government fund would not go directly to the victims. Its purpose is to silence victims with donations from Japanese people and to silence NGOs involved in the human rights of women with ODA funds. Recently, a high official of the government even went so far as to say that, "Japanese ODA reflects the nation's remorse for war and colonial rule, which inflicted damage and pain on Asian nations," a statement that shows an absolute refusal to consider various cases of environmental destruction and human rights violations brought about by Japanese ODA.

A deeply ingrained view held by Japanese men that "comfort women" were licensed prostitutes and were available for money was presented recently in a newspaper column: "There is no progress in continuing to apologize. Not all the former 'comfort women' were forced. I agree that this issue will be settled by paying them some charity money out of 'appreciation and gratitude.'" The article says that Japanese women should also be recipients of this charity money. It is obvious that such a "civil fund" and "charity money" are intended as another humiliation to the dignity of the victims and should never be accepted.

The Japanese government's argument that "compensation was settled by bilateral treaties" easily falls apart when we consider the fact that not even a single word was mentioned about "comfort women" during the negotiations on the Japan-Korea Treaty or the Japan-Philippines Treaty.

But this is a minor point when compared to the question of whether the issue of violation of women's sexuality could be settled between nation-states.

What the victims are saying is the fact that sexual damage cannot be healed unless compensated for individually and that they reject the way that the issue is being utilized as a lever for political and economic negotiations between states.

A point to be noted in considering military sexual slavery by Japan is that when the state of Japan waged aggressive war and violence against another state, a significant portion of its aggressive force took the form of systematic sexual violence against women in the battlefields.

It is highly doubtful whether there are any states that can objectively judge sexual state crimes when these patriarchal societies have let violence exist as a symbol of masculinity and of power. What kind of action should be taken in order to achieve non-violence? We should listen to the voices of the survivors. Not a single breath should be missed. Survivors are demanding that "crimes committed by the Japanese military should be redressed by the Japanese government," and they also insist that to recognize and redress historical mistakes prevents those same mistakes from being repeated.

It is an appeal that also questions whether Japan is really capable of not repeating the same mistakes, when it is becoming involved in United Nations Peace-keeping Forces, aiming for a permanent seat on the UN Security Council, and is therefore not free of the suspicion that it is planning another deployment of its military into Asian countries. In order for Japanese women in our aggressor state to obtain trust, we need to make real apologies and offer compensation for the victims, as well as to create the power to stop Japan's expanding state violence.

Japan's military sexual slavery issues should not be reduced to a mere negotiation lever for states. Beyond state boundaries, women need to create common understanding of each other's history.

8

Commodified Sex (Sexism): Japan's Pornographic Culture

Yunomae Tomoko

Japan's pornographic culture exists in many forms. At one extreme are the straightforward prostitution businesses: "soaplands" (a kind of massage parlor), "date clubs" (where male customers select women from the club either through photos or by looking through a peephole into a room where the women stay, and then set up days), "*hotetoru*" (a kind of call-girl service), clubs, and other services.

One step down from these we find the "fashion health clubs" (where the actual sexual act is not performed), telephone sex clubs, and "*omiai* clubs," where women are invited to drink and eat for free, and where the male customers are invited in by staff members telling them there are women inside, and where the male customers then set up dates with the women in other establishments, with the pub receiving a cut from the money that is exchanged. Then there are the "bloo-sailor shops" (the word originating in a mixture of "bloomer" and "sailor"), where men can buy articles of clothing used by high school students and other women.

On a more popular level, television and radio programs, as well as newspaper and magazine articles, have highly pornographic contents. The language used by the mass media in its commercials and advertisement is sexually discriminatory against women. Comic books, a favorite pastime among all age groups, are often really no more than a succession of pornographic scenes, often violent, with women as the focus. There are also S&M and other kinds of pornographic photo collections. To the list must now be added so-called "adult videos," computer games, and the "miss contests," or beauty contests.

Economic Growth and the Commodification of Sex (Sexism)

The development of this commodification of sex, or pornographic culture, is closely related to the rapid economic growth Japan has experienced since World War II.

The Japanese economy grew quickly with the support of the technological revolution of the late 1950s, and this growth lasted until the oil shock in the early 1970s. This sudden and vigorous growth brought about tremendous changes in Japanese lifestyles. To understand this we need go no further than the subtitle of the *White Paper on Japan's Economy 1961*, which reads, "Consumption Is a Virtue: The Era of Throw-Away Culture Begins." This document set forward the mode of mass production and mass consumption. The mass media developed in tandem with this, flooding the Japanese consciousness with a constant stream of advertising. The result was a tendency among the general public to regard materialism, mammonism, and hedonism as desirable.

With the passage of the Antiprostitution Law in 1956, the mass media appeared to become more restrained. In the 1970s, though, television stations started to broadcast late-night pornographic shows. These programs began, as did popular weekly magazines and evening and "sports" newspapers, to promote tourism overseas, with a focus on prostitution. In the latter half of the 1970s, these media were giving detailed descriptions of where to find prostitutes, and from what kind of variety of women one could choose, as if they were presenting catalogues for products. Beginning in the 1970s, Japanese women were influenced by the Women's Lib movement, which was born out of the Sexual Revolution, which started in the late 1960s in other developed countries. However it was mostly commercialism, not women, who benefited from the "sexual revolution" in this country. It created a market for commercialized sex (sexism) and profited vastly. The situation did not improve after the slowdown in Japanese economic growth following the two oil crises. Rather, this tendency only continued with the advent of prostitution journalism, which made prostitution seem like harmless fun.

In 1980, women activists began criticizing the exploitative nature of the tendency toward commercialized sex (sexism) with ever clearer arguments. The organized showing of a slide show titled "Pornography Is Violence Against Women," which was produced by the Lesbian-Feminist Center, was the beginning. The show made the female audience very aware of the role played by the everyday scene of apparently sophisticated advertisements and women's photographic images in men's magazines, and how they were sending a message that women were sexual objects meant to be watched. The show was one of the driving forces behind the founding of the Tokyo Rape Crisis Center.

It was in the second half of the 1980s that continued criticism of the commodification of sex (sexism) and sexual discrimination helped to place these issues in the spotlight as problems confronting women. That criticism focused nationwide attention in 1989 on then Prime Minister Uno Sosuke's illicit relationship with a former geisha. The woman received ¥3 million from him in exchange for sexual favors and later exposed the relationship. In outrage over this behavior by a national leader, a number of women's organizations confronted him with letters of protest, and local assemblies adopted resolutions demanding his resignation as prime minister. The scandal and social reactions to it were one reason for the crushing defeat the Liberal Democratic Party suffered in the following Upper House elections. Uno was forced to resign. It was virtually unheard of in Japanese political circles, which is a typical example of male society, for this kind of matter (relationships with a woman) to interfere in the career of a big politician like Uno. There is a traditional saying, "a man's character should not be judged from below the bellybutton," meaning that a man's character is seen as having nothing to do with what he does with women sexually.

The following describes some of the prominent forms of commercialized sex (sexism) and sexual discrimination.

1) "Sports Papers" and Men's Magazines

The Women's Action Group, which was organized in 1975, held a meeting that became the starting point for much of the antipornography movement in Japan. The meeting was titled "Is Rush Hour a Porno Hour? No to Erotic, Gross Sports Papers in Front of Our Eyes!" Every day on trains and buses, commuting women are forced to stand or sit next to men reading "sports papers" (evening tabloids that focus on sports, scandals, and sex) full of obscene photographs of women and extensive articles on the subject of sex. These articles often provide information regarding various sex businesses, and these businesses feed the advertising media. Of course, pornographic articles are not central to the sports papers, but by flooding them with information and advertisements, the sex industry creates a market and a demand for its services.

While the sports papers, which are sold almost exclusively at station kiosks, contain obscene photos and articles, the mainstream newspapers delivered to homes do not. Men who are exhausted from long working hours and long commutes are supposed to be able to take a small break from their stressful life as they read the tabloids. In Japan, there is no minimum age for purchasing these prostitution-driven papers and magazines at station kiosks. The fact that the men who consume these products do not hesitate to be seen reading them in public, and even in front of women, amazes many visitors from other countries. The Women's Action Group organized efforts to condemn this treatment of both the women who appear in the papers and those who are forced to watch men reading them. There was a great response throughout Japan, and this effort was reported overseas as well. Since then, the pornographic articles in some sports papers have been moved from the outside to the inside pages.

In 1993, a popular youth monthly called *Big Tomorrow* featured a cover story which was both vulgar and sexually harassing, outlining how to force an unwilling female co-worker to have sex in the office and how to coerce her into nonresistance. Immediately protests were sent to the publisher by the Women's Network Fighting Against Sexual Violence '90 (STON '90). They condemned the article as glorifying and encouraging sexual harassment, including rape. Some corporations withdrew their advertisements to the magazine, fearing embarrassment when the mass media took up the story. The publishing company ended up acknowledging the problematic nature of the article and met with STON '90 to discuss the matter. The editing staff admitted not having considered the point of view of women and their feelings. Afterwards, recalling the meeting, they gave the impression that the women from STON '90 were not so "out of the ordinary," despite expectations that they would be militant. The publisher held an educational class on discrimination with members of STON '90 as lecturers.

2) Sexually Discriminatory Posters

In various posters advertising products and services, nude women or women in swimsuits are used as eye-catchers. In some cases, an emphasis on a particular part of the body fills an entire ad. Since 1988, women's organizations have been made very busy by the overwhelming amount of these kinds of posters, which themselves constitute sexual harassment.

In publicity posters, most banks have used women in bathing suits, sometimes in an unnatural pose at a swimming pool. One liquor company's ad showed a mud-smeared, prostrate woman with unfocused eyes. She appears as though she had just been raped. A television commercial aired at night from the same company, with the same model, portrayed her being teased by cowboys circling her on horses. The protests from women's groups resulted in a discontinuation of the commercial and the removal of the posters. The major advertising agency which produced the ad and the commercial set up a monitoring system to have consumers approve its products.

One poster advocating the usefulness of the Tokyo subway system to foreigners featured a close-up of the calves of a woman wearing red high heels. After protests by women's groups, some of the posters were removed. The Women's Action Group started an antipornography campaign in which they put a sticker with the Chinese character for "anger" on posters they came across. The Japan Women's Studies Society in 1988 chose the theme "politics of the visual image" for its conference, and analyzed depictions of women in the mass media. Their tactic was to put a sticker reading, "This Is Discrimination Against Women," on posters deserving the label.

Women were outraged by the appearance of one men's clothing ad showing a woman in a man's coat, laying on the ground barefoot, with her wrists tied behind her back. The major advertising agency Dentsu, which produced it, discussed the matter with the protesting women and decided to hold an in-house human rights education class with lecturers from the Women's Action Group.

It is not only posters by big corporations that have the tendency to discriminate against women. Japan's biggest labor union, Rengo, made an advocacy poster calling for participation in its May Day activities. It featured the body of a woman in a skimpy swimsuit and the catchphrase "Space for Workers" printed on her bust. Another set of problematic advocacy posters was created in 1991 for a campaign conducted by the Prevention of AIDS Foundation affiliated with the Ministry of Health and Welfare. One poster featured a man covering his face with a Japanese passport, with only his grinning mouth visible. The poster read, "Go have a good time! . . . and take care not to get AIDS." Another poster showed a miniature naked woman trapped in a condom. Women spoke out against these posters, as they spread the message that it was acceptable for Japanese men to buy women overseas and that they seemed to make women, not men, the source of the deadly virus. In 21 administrative divisions throughout Japan, both types of posters were withdrawn from circulation.

3) Beauty Contests

The year 1990 saw active arguments over beauty contests. It all began with a protest by the Council of Sakai Women's Organization over a planned contest, "The World Contest for the Miss Flower Pageant," which was to take place as part of the Flower and Green Exposition in Osaka. The council came up with a number of methods to question the purpose and conduct of the contest.

First, questionnaires regarding how beauty contests were conducted and their contents were sent out to all 3,382 local governments throughout Japan. They found that 70.1% of all local governments sponsored beauty contests in one way or another. Eighty percent of the judges were male, and there were no concrete criteria for selection. The detailed findings were put together in a book, *No to Beauty Contests!*

The council also held two protest rallies with some 2,000 participants. In order to reveal the discriminatory and deceptive nature of beauty contests, the protesters sponsored a male version of a beauty contest as a parody. Under the pressure of these women's actions, the sponsor for the beauty contest at the exposition decided not to officially announce the contestants' bust, waist, and hip measurements. Osaka Prefecture dropped its sponsorship, and the expected entrants from New Zealand canceled their participation.

Similarly, in Tokyo, a series of protests against the Tokyo Beauty Contest, which was sponsored by the *Tokyo Shimbun* (a daily paper), were initiated. Five activist contestants, including Mitsui Mariko, a member of the Tokyo metropolitan assembly, tried to enter the contest to raise questions. Tokyo withdrew its sponsorship, and the governor of Tokyo resigned as a judge.

The movement to denounce beauty contests spread throughout

Japan, and 25 local governments have discontinued the contests since then. This movement is a way of questioning many aspects of beauty contests: the made-up standards of feminine beauty; the internalization of these standards by women themselves; the narrowly defined value of women demonstrated by these superficial competitions; the objectification of women, the idealization of European-type beauty; the power structure between the two sexes, women's labor and wage problems, etc. Women as well as men reacted to this movement, and the mass media paid a great deal of attention to the controversy.

4) Porno Videos

Leaflets and free catalogues for porno videos are widely distributed to homes in the suburbs. Those cast in the videos include junior and senior high school students. There are hardcore porno videos called "*ura-video*," or underground videos. The intimate relationship between pornography and violence and violence-related crime was revealed in 1987 when a man was killed at a Ikebukuro hotel as a result of an obsession he had with videotaping his sexual assaults on prostitutes. He threatened one with a knife while intending to videotape the abuse, but was stabbed to death by his own knife. Everything was taped by the video camera he had set up.

This case involved many factors, such as prostitution and violence, women's sexual freedom, and other issues surrounding prostitution. The most outstanding point was the discrimination against a woman who was working as a prostitute. Women activists supported the defendant because she had acted out of self-defense. In a review by an appellate court, the judge gave her a suspended sentence, ending the trial. Unable to distinguish between the real and the unreal, the man who died had tried to play out his fantasy through the use of violence, a woman, and a video camera.

In 1992, the AV (adult video = porno video) Human Rights Network was founded after revelations that one video had used actual rape scenes. The network's activities include calling attention to violations of human rights, such as involuntary performances and breaches of contract by producers. The group has set up telephone counseling services for victimized women.

A Huge Industry

Our daily life is inundated with commercialized sex (sexism) and pornographic culture, and recent women's protests only scratch the surface of this sexploitation. According to recent statistics, sex industry profits amount to ¥500 billion.

The purpose of the 1956 Antiprostitution Law was to prohibit managed prostitution and to protect women's welfare, but the law provides punishment only against prostitutes walking the streets. Consequently, the law does not fit the reality of today's varied and diversified forms of prostitution. Another problem regarding the Law is raised from the viewpoint of sexual equality. The Child Welfare Law, which deals with juvenile prostitution, is also problematic in terms of how it views sexual equality. The juvenile prostitute broker is punished and the girl is put into protection, but there is no punishment against the man who pays.

From 1990 to 1991, attention was focused on the problem of "bad-influence (pornographic) comics." Mothers claimed that pornographic comics were a bad influence on youth and initiated a joint campaign focused on local authorities, publishers, bookstores and the police, which spread throughout the country. Consequently the publishers began to voluntarily regulate their comics to avoid police investigation and punishment. The notion of the "commodification of sex" was incorporated into the philosophy of "moralistic social purification," undermining feminist protests against both regulation and sexist expression. During that period the Life and Culture Bureau of the Tokyo Metropolitan government released its "Research on the Commodification of Sex," which examined sexual expressions in 1,221 comics. As the mass media reported these results with great interest, it was said that the research by Tokyo would lead to regulations against "bad-influence comics."

Since 1989 the term "commodification of sex" has become common and has come to be an important topic because of the influence of the women's movement. Progressive male intellectuals as well as men's magazines, however, have condemned the antipornography campaign, insisting on "freedom of expression." Others claimed that in capitalist society all things are commodified, and sex is no exception. Consequently, sexploitation is a small problem. This confusion between "sexual expression" and "sexist expression" clearly shows how difficult it is to achieve recognition of the concept of sexual discrimination. The notion of the "commodification of sex" is complicated by the diversification of ideas on women's sexuality, new theories on "pornography by women (acceptable for women)," "the happy commodification of sex," and "the personal choice to sell sex."

9

Promoting Prostitution

Okura Yayoi

In September 1994, a group of four Japanese freelance writers calling themselves the "Asian Sexual Customs Study Group" published a controversial book entitled *Tai Baishun Tokuhon* (Thailand Prostitution Handbook). The guidebook describes in detail the places and prices at which they actually bought women in Thailand, the types of women they found, the conversations they had, and the sex acts they performed. It provides a map showing practically every place where sex can be bought—go-go bars, massage parlors, coffee shops in Bangkok hotels, and brothels in Chiang Mai. Photographs of Thai women adorn almost every page.

The preface reads, arrogantly, "Some may criticize us, but prostitution or the buying and selling of sex is one type of encounter between a man and a woman. Mediation by booze and money does not stop it from being a meeting of persons. This book reports on actual experiences, the results of almost too earnest a search for this type of encounter." In the end, however, the book evidently proves to be nothing but a guidebook to buying women.

The book can be found at both major and neighborhood bookstores in Japan, alongside economic and political commentaries on Asia, reports on the area's social conditions, and travel journals. In Bangkok, it is available at bookstores which deal in Japanese books. The first 15,000 copies appear to have almost sold out within just five months.

In the 1970s, Japanese men's sex tours attracted much attention. They were usually arranged and offered by regular travel agencies in package tours: sightsee during the day and devour women at night. Popular destinations were South Korea, Taiwan, the Philippines, and Thailand. Thronging together to buy women, Japanese men were a strange sight in the region.

In the meantime, women's groups in these countries began protesting against Japanese men's sex tours and called Japanese men "sex animals." In Japan as well, women's groups started protest movements and succeeded in putting the issue on the agenda of the National Diet. Tourist bureaus gradually began to refrain from advertising such tours. But this was in no way associated with a decrease in the number of Japanese men going abroad to buy sex.

Then in the mid-1980s Japan became involved in international trafficking in women. Procured by the yakuza, Asian women have been brought to Japan and made to work in the sex industry. For Japanese men, this means they no longer have to go overseas to purchase Thai and Filipino women because they are at home. Today, it is estimated that over one hundred thousand foreign women are working in the sex industry in Japan.

The attitude of Japanese men is the same whether they buy women abroad or at home. The arrogant assumption that women are mere servants to men's sexuality and that Asian women easily succumb to the lure of money (the yen) has not changed. This men's arrogance is the same underlying attitude which produced the military "comfort women" system.

The Double Meaning of *Baishun*

In the book's title, *Tai Baishun Tokuhon,* the word *baishun,* meaning prostitution, needs some explanation. The word is written with two Chinese characters, which together mean literally "selling spring" (meaning the season). Spring connotes sex or women's bodies. Thus, the word emphasized women selling their bodies. It was during the anti-sex tour movement of the 1970s that a new awareness was developed. The main problem came to be seen not as women who sell their bodies, but men who buy women. Thus, a new combination of characters for the word prostitution was introduced—"buying spring." Since the pronunciations of the Chinese characters "sell" and "buy" are the same, the new word retained the same pronunciation but took on a new meaning which focused on men as consumers. Women activists promoted the use of this new version of the word, and today the expression is listed in one of the most authoritative and popular Japanese dictionaries.

It is this new combination of characters that is used to write *baishun* in the title of the book. The word, which was originally used to criticize men's buying, is now blatantly used to promote the act, illustrating the horrible degree of their insensitivity, self-justification, and malicious intent.

Immediately, women's groups and anti-child prostitution groups charged the publisher with promoting sex tourism and demanded that it withdraw the book from circulation. However, the publisher replied that it had no intention of encouraging sex tourism and that the book merely reported on the realities, and went on to say that it was not its responsibility should the book instigate the readers to buy sex.

The way Japanese people travel is changing as we gain more experience in traveling abroad. While many Japanese like to travel on group tours, there has been an increase in people who prefer traveling alone. This also applies to sex tourism. Group sex tours appear to be on the wane. But all the same, Japanese men are heading out to Asian countries for sex, alone or in small groups, so they appear to be on a regular or business trip. It is difficult to obtain exact numbers on men who buy women abroad, but a look at tourism statistics variegated by gender and destination indicates the trends. Among those who traveled to Taiwan, 550,000 were men, while 170,000 were women; for

South Korea, the figures were 960,000 and 340,000; and to Thailand, 240,000 and 130,000. The case of the Philippines is overwhelming—170,000 men and only 30,000 women, or less than 20% of the number of male tourists (*Immigration Statistics Annual,* 1993). Without such a backdrop the Thai prostitution handbook could never have been published or sold so many copies.

In January 1995, the Thai foreign minister expressed his displeasure and issued a protest statement against the book. The Thai embassy in Japan also issued a statement and expressed its unhappiness with the book. Sixteen Thai NGOs have sent a joint protest letter to the publisher. Meanwhile, however, the publisher has moved ahead with plans for a second printing. Neither the publisher nor the writers are concerned that the book will aggravate the prejudice in Japanese society against Thai women, which equates them with prostitutes, or damage Thai people's pride. What they also miss, however, is that the book has turned out to be an excellent revelation of the disgusting stupidity of Japanese men.

10

The Trafficking of Women

Murata Noriko

In Japan, the term "foreign migrant women" is often used to designate Asian women who have come here from their home countries to work, engaging mainly in the so-called "sex industry." There are more than 100,000 foreign women working in this industry. They occupy the lowest rung of an enormous, lucrative business that brings in trillions of yen a year. Many of them are sent to Japan by human smuggling gangs—crime syndicates that force them to work as prostitutes or sex slaves.

During the latter half of the 1960s and throughout the 1970s, many Japanese men went on sex tours to Southeast Asia, where they could buy sex. The first target was Taiwan, where Japanese was still understood due to fifty years of colonial rule. As Japan entered a period of high economic growth, overseas tours became more and more popular. In 1972, when flights between Taiwan and Japan were temporarily shut down as the result of normalization of Japan-China relations, South Korea became the new target. Kieseng (Korean girl) tours quickly became the rage among sightseeing tours. Japanese men, whose reputation as enterprise warriors earned them the appellation "economic animals," came to be called by a new name—"sex animals."

Following the lead of Korean women who were protesting the use of economic power (yen) by Japanese men to dehumanize their sisters, Japanese women also started to take action against the Kieseng tours. Despite these protest movements, sex tourism by Japanese males expanded, in the late 1970s, to Southeast Asia, particularly the Philippines and Thailand. The anti-sex tourism movement also spread throughout Asia. Japanese politicians were confronted by a chain of protest actions when they visited affected countries, and the situation was broadcast all over the world, making Japanese men's "prostitute-buying tours" to East and Southeast Asia a subject of national and international scorn.

Syndicates Emerge

In the early 1980s sex tourism to Southeast Asia continued, though less openly. Around this time women from the Philippines began to be sent to Japan. Some came to work legally as singers or dancers on an entertainer/artist visa, but many were sent by human smuggling gangs who had connections with Japanese yakuza, or organized crime syndicates. Human rights violations committed against these women, such as confinement, violence and forced prostitution, increased.

Since the mid-1980s, the number of Thai women coming to Japan has increased. Nowadays, more than 100,000 Asian women are sent to Japan each year to work in the sex industry. Most come from Thailand and the Philippines.

Many find it impossible to escape from forced prostitution at small bars (called *snacks*) or regular bars in city red light districts or at local hot spring resorts. An especially large number of Thai women are tricked into coming to Japan by agents working for local and international human smuggling gangs. They are lured by promises of jobs in factories and told that they will be able to pay their debts off in a very short time, send considerable amounts of money home to their families, and make their parents happy.

Upon arrival in Japan they are sold to the yakuza or snack owners at the price of nearly ¥4 million and their passports and identification cards are taken away. This is when they realize that they have been deceived. At this point, however, they are already under close watch by the gangsters. They cannot go out freely, let alone escape, until they finish paying off all their fictitious and inflated debts. In this way, a Japan that boasts of peace and prosperity also allows the existence of what can fairly be called a system of modern sexual slavery.

According to statistics from the Immigration Bureau, each year as many as 55,000 "undocumented" Thai women overstay their visas and remain in Japan. Compared with women from the Philippines, Thai women are more liable to become victims of exploitation and violence. Most come from rural communities and cannot speak any English. They come to Japan on tourist visas and work under conditions of undocumented residence and labor. Unfortunately, women from Buddhist countries cannot turn to Japanese temples for help in the same way that Filipinas can turn to Catholic churches.

In the early 1990s there were several cases where Thai women trying to escape from situations of confinement and forced prostitution killed their shop owners or managers, who, in the majority of cases, were other Asian women. They committed murder out of desperation, seeing no other way out of their situation.

Who Should Be on Trial?

In September 1991, in Shimodate City, Ibaragi Prefecture, three Thai women who were forced into prostitution killed their boss, who was also Thai, and escaped with a bag that contained their passports. It also contained millions of yen in cash and jewelry. They were arrested on charges of "robbery and murder." Murder for money is a grave crime in Japan. It can lead to a sentence of life imprisonment or the death penalty. The court chose to ignore the circumstances of confinement and forced prostitution and sentenced them to ten years in prison in a trial that took two and a half years to conclude. After painful deliberation the women decided to appeal to a higher court on the grounds that they were not thieves, but were defending their dignity as human beings.

Several other murders have occurred involving circumstances similar to those of the Shimodate case. In most cases the final judgment has been handed down without any understanding of the cruel treatment these women endure, the smuggling, confinement, violence, sexual abuse, and forced prostitution that brings them to the point where they dare to commit murder.

There are important questions that need to be asked. Who should be on trial? The women who have been sexually enslaved or the criminal smugglers who make enormous gains by exploiting them? Don't the men who buy prostitutes, who regard women only as sexual commodities, bear any responsibility?

A Thai woman who was accused in one of these murder cases wrote a letter to the Embassy of Thailand in Tokyo, concerned about other Thai women who want to come to Japan to work. The letter explained the situation as follows:

"There are no factories where we can work, there are only bars and pubs and men who only think about drinking and having sex. I really suffered a lot. We had to go to bed with dirty men and strangers. If you don't do whatever you are told to do, you are beaten by the boss or the proprietress (*mama-san*).

For them we Thai women are mere animals. They have the power of life and death over us. Japan is not heaven but hell for us Thai women. It's a barefaced lie that the cherry blossoms are waiting for you. What is waiting for you are men whose only concern is having sex.

No matter how hard you work, putting your life on the line, there are no rewards, not even a single baht. If you don't obey them, they'll hit you, beat you, and do whatever they want. To them, we have no value other than that of a tool they use to make money by entertaining drunks and providing sex.

Japan is not a place for Thai women who are eager to work. Please stay in Thailand. In our country people still have sympathy. No matter how much you have to suffer, no matter how hard you have to work, it's far better than being trapped in hell like me."

No End of Consumerism

Faced with the prospect of enforced prostitution, anguish and other serious problems like drug dependency, gambling and mental collapse, some women consider suicide their only alternative.

Especially in recent years, as the immigration authorities have tightened controls, fear of deportation has deterred many of these women from seeking help from public offices or the police department when they are treated unjustly or are in bad health. Some manage to flee to NGOs who support foreign laborers or to private shelters. Others are so closely guarded that they cannot escape. As these women are increasingly confined, their problems are less and less visible, and their situation becomes increasingly dangerous. Asian women are used to fill up a labor shortage caused by the expansion of the sex industry.

The number of Asian migrant women who give birth in Japan has also increased as more settle here or stay longer. But precise numbers and details about their situation are difficult to obtain as many have overstayed their visas and are therefore in the country illegally. There are many cases where children are abandoned without any identification, thus becoming stateless.

As the situation of Thai and Filipina women smuggled into Japan illustrates, there are people who make a huge amount of money from smuggling, who discriminate against and disdain Asian women, and who buy prostitutes, injuring them both spiritually and physically. These people are the very same Japanese men who are called enterprise warriors, the human smugglers, or yakuza.

Trafficking in women and mistreatment of women migrants are products of the economic disparity between Japan and neighboring Asian countries; the Japanese government's continuing policy of exclusion toward foreign workers; and the intersection of racism, sexism and consumer capitalism that makes Japanese men believe that they can simply buy women from poor countries with money, in Japan or abroad. Their arrogance and lack of any consideration for the rights of Asian women to live in dignity and free from bondage make them the object of scorn and criticism.

11

In Search of Ruby Moreno

Ann Kaneko

Representations of non-Japanese ethnic groups in Japanese popular media are few and far between. In fact, I am sure it is possible to count on two hands the cumulative number of films from the past five years focusing on non-Japanese communities in Japan.

Among these, the Ruby Moreno "series" stands out prominently. Moreno, a Filipina actress based in Japan, starred in three films portraying Filipinas between 1992 and 1993: *Tsuki wa dotchi ni deteiru* (Which Side Is the Moon on, 1993), *Afureru atsui namida* (Swimming in Tears, 1992), and the Fuji Television drama *Fuiripina wo aishita otokotachi* (Men Who Loved Filipinas, 1992).

No doubt Moreno owes her popularity to the establishment of the Filipino community in Japan and the canonization of the Filipina hostess as part of Japan's seedy sex industry. Aside from the older, more established Korean and Chinese communities, Filipinos are probably the senior members of Japan's "newcomer" Asian groups. Filipinas outnumber men in Japan, and many work as hostesses and entertainers.

I propose to look at the Moreno films as well as *Tsuma wa fuiripina* (My Wife Is Filipina, 1992), a documentary focusing on a Japanese-Filipina couple. By examining these films, I hope to gain a better understanding of how Japanese society views Filipinas and how these kinds of media serve in reinforcing these images.

Stereotyping Filipinas

Strongly influenced by the notion of multiculturalism in the United States, I am particularly curious as to how these same ideas hold up within the context of, say, a society like Japan which has traditionally been ethnically closed and isolated. Judging from the situation of Korean-Japanese, Japan, too, has a history of ethnic diversity, but it is hesitant to formulate a public policy which acknowledges this situation. Consequently, immigration laws have not changed, and the current wave of undocumented and documented workers from surrounding Asian countries and Nikkei (Japanese descendants) from Latin America are treated in much the same way as the Korean forced laborers who came to Japan 70 years earlier.

Viewing these films, I was struck by the fact that in all of them, the Filipinas are (except in *Namida,* in which Moreno is a *"hanayome-san,"* a woman who has come to Japan to marry a Japanese farmer) hostesses or entertainers (and at times prostitutes). I suppose that for those living in Japan, this is not surprising since that is the general perception of Filipinas. Despite the reality that the main profession available to Filipinas in Japan is in *"mizu shobai"* (entertainment work), there are also a fair number of women who work in small factories, as domestic helpers, are married to Japanese or are here to study. Given these circumstances, at what point does the image of the Filipina hostess become a stereotype? Why do producers choose to popularize this image, reinforcing this stereotype? I cannot help wondering whether producers as well as Japanese audience members realize that this image of Filipinas is the product of the specialized role that these women are allowed to hold within this society and certainly not one of their own choosing. I wonder how many uncritical viewers fail to understand or analyze this situation, assuming that all Filipinas (both here and in the Philippines) do this kind of work.

This claim of stereotyping was a main complaint of Filipinas living in Japan speaking out against the television drama *Otokotachi.* In 1993, Liza Go, senior secretary at the Hiroshima Peace and Human Rights Center of the National Christian Council in Japan (NCC), led a group of Filipinas who protested this drama, describing it as "discriminatory." The first issue of the Thinking about Media and Human Rights Group's newsletter outlined the main complaints of these women: (1) Filipinas are stereotypically portrayed as deceptive, opportunistic, money-hungry hostess/prostitutes who willingly jump into bed for their own financial advancement. In addition, the meaner personality traits of Ruby (the hostess played by Moreno), the main character, may be viewed as characteristic of all Filipinas. (2) Japanese media commonly use Smoky Mountain and Ermita as locations to represent the Philippines showing only its extreme poverty or its seedier side. (3) The last scene, when Ruby, Toshio (Moreno's boyfriend, played by a Japanese actor) and his mother are tossing candy and rice to the poor of Smoky Mountain, is irresponsible and patronizing. (4) The halting Japanese used by Ruby and the coarse Tagalog used by Toshio are also prejudicial, making Ruby appear to be no more than an imbecile, unable to adequately express herself in Japanese.

One viewing of this drama demonstrates that the claims of these women are valid. In fact, the same has been said in the past about much programming in the United States. By simply exchanging ethnic group, character, locale and language, one could be talking about a number of other shows. None of their claims are new or surprising—except that they are being raised in Japan.

Stereotyping Japanese

However, perhaps what they fail to mention is that not only is the Filipina character caricatured and one-sided but so are the Japanese characters. Toshio is no beacon of responsibility or intelligence and appears to be extremely naive. I think most Japanese would strongly resent being equated with him. Toshio's mother's character, so willing to move to the Philippines, is also highly implausible. I cannot take this program seriously. Of course, this does not lessen the seriousness of its offenses toward the Philippine community. Because of the lack of Filipina representation in general, the influence of this kind of drama has a greater effect than it normally would in forming preconceptions of Filipinas. In the case of Japanese, there are other portraits to balance these representations, but there are only few other depictions of Filipinas. Consequently, these images carry much more weight.

Another element which the Filipinas' group failed to mention, but is painfully obvious to me is the tendency to want to patronize Ruby—the poor Filipina who comes to earn money to support her family. She's "*kawaiso*" (pitiful). By distancing the audience with sympathy, it is easier not to take responsibility for the reality that she faces and that is, in turn, the responsibility of the system which put her in such a situation.

The program is also guilty of trying superficially to pack in all elements of Philippine-Japanese history. That Ruby's father had suffered at the hands of Japanese seems like yet another fact that they wanted to "squeeze in" so that they would receive higher marks on their report card for Philippine-Japanese history.

The degree to which the drama in its entirety is far-fetched and one-sided makes me take a more radical position toward the validity of a business which commodifies and packages stories with so little resonance with reality. It is clear that the story blends intrigue and romance and has all of the dramatic elements necessary for television—yakuza underworld, boy meets girl, overcoming odds, Cinderella rags to riches. Consequently this story was produced because these elements fulfill the needs of dramatic storytelling rather than any interest in rendering truthful or sympathetic portraits of these women or of the reality they face day to day.

Unfortunately, much of the same can be said for Moreno's character in *Tsuki*. This time, she is a little more savvy, speaking in fast-paced, sophisticated Kansai dialect. Despite the efforts of the film's Korean-Japanese makers at tackling the larger issues of race relations in Japan, especially dealing with the situation of Korean-Japanese, their own limited vision of Filipinas prompts them to present a rather stereotypic view of them, no different from the images produced by their Japanese counterparts. Although it is a harder look and is less patronizing, Moreno's character is still the caricatured, streetwise and determined hostess, quite adept at using people to get her way.

In *Namida,* Moreno is plain, without makeup and in simple clothes. Faye (played by Moreno) escapes her husband for Tokyo. The isolated life of rural drudgery is difficult for her to bear, and she wants to go home to her mother in the Philippines. Unlike in the other dramas, she is not a hostess involved in the sex industry. Yet in this film, everything is dark and grim. It is hard for me to believe that she could be so solemn. I do not doubt the possibility that she could be so isolated and lonely, but it seems that the makers are afflicted with a kind of patronizing attitude which, in some ways, is equally damaging. In this film, they seem to say, "Look at the plight of the poor Filipina *hanayome-san.*"

Perhaps the biggest drawback of the film is the parallel story of her Japanese neighbors, Asami and Shuichi. They are involved in a violent, masochistic relationship which is supposed to somehow echo the sexual violence in the society. However, it does not ring true. Instead the film seems fractured into two stories which have little to do with each other Faye's story and theirs. Although the film is careful to separate Faye from the image of the stereotypic hostess, juxtaposing her with her neighbors almost seems to associate her by default with that from which the filmmakers try to disassociate her.

In this film as well, there is an attempt to take a glimpse at the larger cross-section of foreigners living in Japan. At the Chinese restaurant in Tokyo where Faye takes refuge, working as a waitress, as her friend Maria did before her, many "*gaikokujin*" (foreigners) gather from many countries to spend lighter moments, drinking and talking. Yet in this restaurant, one sees no Japanese and Westerners who come to work at white-collar jobs; day laborers and students mingle freely—quite unlikely.

The Filipina drama does not end in the theaters or on television. For Moreno, the details of her private life were spilled out onto the covers of the tabloids. She revealed that she had also come to Japan to work in the entertainment trade for money, that she was older than she had publicly said she was, that she was supporting a handicapped child in the Philippines. In a sense, the media tried to make her acknowledge that she was like the characters she played in the films—a little deceptive, determined and in need of yen. However, this all seemed to me to be a greater indication of the degree to which she is at the mercy of the business that employs her. It wants her to be like the characters she plays. Despite these pressures, Moreno can be commended for her courage in being critical of the typecast roles which she is forced to play, stating that she wants to play different roles and develop as an actress.

Of these films, it would seem most likely that *My Wife Is Filipina* would be the closest to presenting elements of the truth since it is a *documentary* based on reality. Yet, in fact, it could be the most problematic because viewers might be less apt to be critical of it because it supposedly is a depiction of reality. Terada Yasunori, the director and a film student at the time, decided to document his marriage and experiences living with Theresa, a Filipina he met at a Filipina pub, making it his thesis film. Theirs is a shotgun marriage, and Theresa has gone back to Manila while she awaits the birth of their child and Terada in the Philippines to marry her. Since the film is a personal documentary about the relationship between the director and Theresa, perhaps its greatest value is its insight into Terada and his family, not its depiction of Theresa. Of his family, only his sister is an active and willing participant, who goes with her brother to witness his wedding. At the beginning of the film, Terada states that he was involved with three other Filipinas before meeting Theresa. He admits his obsession with Filipinas, no doubt similar to that of other Japanese men. Although he is marrying Theresa, it does not seem that he knows her very well, understands her economic responsibilities or her reason for being in Japan. He questions Shirley, a friend of Theresa's who is married to Yabu-san, another Japanese man, and her answers are guarded. He unabashedly asks Shirley, "Did you marry him for his money? "Would you have married him if he did not promise to build you a house in Manila?" "Did you love him when you married him?" She smiles in embarrassment when she answers. It seems clear that marriage for her is a practical choice, representing economic stability and a means of supporting her family, not a question of romance.

In his own relationship with Theresa, he does not understand why she must work to support her family, why she wants to send her daughter Yoko back to Manila so that she can work full-time, or why her brother does not work in Manila. He is condescending when he speaks to her and her answers are guarded. In one scene, she openly encourages him to leave her and remarry a Japanese woman who would presumably better fulfill his expectations. Instead of providing understanding, it seems that the film raises more questions as to why he does not understand. And of course, there is the fundamental question as to why he and so many other Japanese men are so attracted to Filipinas. For Theresa, her sexuality and ability to serve men are what she has to sell, and Terada was and, in some ways, continues to be the buyer. Their personal lives mimic the economic relations between the two countries from which they come.

At a November 1994 "international exchange" panel discussion after a screening of his film, Terada said that he decided to make the film because media coverage dealing with Filipinas seemed extremely different from his personal experiences with Filipinas around him. Yet it seems to me that his documentary fails to show anything more than the perception of Filipinas in Japan, probably due to his own lack of understanding. Indeed, many Filipinos and Filipinas who viewed the documentary with me expressed their concern that Theresa might be considered representative of all Filipinas living in Japan.

I also find it curious that Japanese critics have recognized and awarded *Tsuki* and *Filipina* to the extent that they have. *Tsuki* swept many of the major critics awards in 1994, and *Filipina* received prizes at both the 1992 International Student Film Festival and a Japanese Director's Guild Young Director's award. It seems both have been acknowledged because of the topics that they attempt to deal with and the lack of other noteworthy films rather than on the merit of the films themselves.

Coming from Los Angeles where there is a large, well-established Filipino community, it is difficult for me to accept these stereotypic perceptions of Filipinas in Japan without being highly critical. So prevalent are these ideas that a close Filipina friend in Los Angeles refuses to visit Japan for fear of being mistaken as an entertainer and looked down on accordingly.

Increasing numbers of media makers and critics of different ethnic backgrounds emerge in the "multicultural" melting pot of the United States. Consequently, representation of these different groups is no longer taken at "face" value. Especially since the consciousness-raising of the 1960s and 1970s, stereotypical depictions of African Americans, Native Americans, Asian Americans and Latin Americans have been questioned and reevaluated. Although one-sided depictions still persist, overt caricatures are less prevalent; and, in general, there is some heed paid to avoid stepping on the toes of certain more prominent ethnic communities. Most importantly, these groups are now in a better position to portray themselves and those who choose to portray them are forced to do more homework.

As many in liberal circles subscribe to "political correctness," commercial media makers necessarily make more of an effort not to offend, making sure that depictions fall within the realm of what is acceptable. It's a cat-and-mouse game of avoiding bad press. I certainly do not propose this kind of superficial lip service as an appropriate solution. Yet this is no doubt part of the slow process of working toward greater awareness.

The face of Japanese society is changing slowly, especially since the bubble years, when many new faces appeared in urban areas. Yet despite the efforts of the society to make it an uncomfortable stay for these visitors, many of Japan's new residents have learned the language, married Japanese, and have children who speak only Japanese. In view of the coming generations of children with mixed identity, it is to be hoped that the new complexity of the society will begin to be reflected in the sophistication of the representation of its different members. Perhaps marginalized segments of this society will gain power and begin to be able to represent themselves, taking on the role of providing greater balance in the programming produced by the current financial and political powers which control the media. I am hopeful that one day, in Japan, I will be able to meet the real Ruby Moreno.

12

Lesbians and Sexual Self-Determination

Hara Minako

As a 38-year-old lesbian with a child, I have taken part for the past ten years or so in work to create a safer space for lesbians in Tokyo. If it has become easier for women to love women during these ten years, it is because self-identified lesbians and bisexual women have emerged to work on lesbian issues, whether in lesbian-only groups, with gay men, or in other women's groups.

Lesbians are now finally acquiring a voice of our own instead of being addressed as pitiful victims or as an invisible minority. Over 20 grassroots groups and newsletters for lesbian/bisexual women now exist in the Tokyo area. Many of them have been started recently by younger women. At least ten major cities throughout Japan have one or more lesbian/gay groups.

Sexual self-determination is, naturally, a major issue for any lesbian, as it is for any woman, but it is not possible to get people to yearn for something that they have never known. Although an increasing number of straight women are beginning to accept the fact that women may love other women at some point in our lives, they are still slow to see the connection between the lesbian struggle for sexual self-determination and their own fears of unwanted pregnancies. Most people think they are doing us a gracious favor just by tolerating our presence. Many of the social problems lesbians face are shared by all single women—low wages outside the home, jobs with no prospects, and economic dependence on parents.

Perhaps as in any other country, the battle for women's sexual self-determination in Japan must begin in the home. Fear of parental disapproval is a primary obstacle stopping lesbians from coming out, especially for younger women who reside with their families. This may be invisible from the outside, but is strong enough to keep young women in the closet. Mothers typically check their daughter's mail or diaries, so if a young woman is subscribing to a lesbian newsletter, she lives under the constant fear of discovery. This is why we commonly receive requests asking us to send newsletters in plain envelopes.

Single women over the age of 30 commonly end up becoming unpaid caretakers for male family members and aging parents. At the same time, people may consider them less than complete "women" because they do not have any children.

Another big obstacle to people coming out is heterosexual marriage, which is commonly considered an obligation rather than a right. Heterosexual marriage is a highly discriminatory practice that reinforces classism, racism, able-ism, ageism and sexism, but it is also an extremely practical social arrangement that seems to offer the emotional security of being "just like everyone else."

Sex within marriage is the only socially acknowledged form of public female sexual expression. Historically, women have been allowed to express themselves sexually only with their own husbands, within the limits of marriage, pregnancy and childbirth, always in that order.

Heterosexual marriage has become the easiest way for women to stay away from undesirable harassment, especially when they are pregnant. The procedures are so simple. Marrying a person of the right sex, class, nationality (Japanese), and physical ability, brings substantial legal, financial and social privilege.

Marriage is also common because, most parents insist that it is their "obligation" to marry off their daughter and claim that they have the "right" to see the faces of their grandchildren. I have seen many women in rural areas, as well as women from well-to-do families, succumb to the pressure of marriage after some years of resistance.

Marriage out of desperation, however, often leads to depression, marital conflict, extramarital affairs, and violent retaliation by angry husbands. The issue becomes more complicated when a married woman becomes involved in a relationship with another woman. This is the area where a lesbian woman is most vulnerable to male violence and needs urgent legal assistance, because even when the husband becomes physically violent, virtually no one takes the woman's side. Heterosexual marriage openly justifies sanctions against any voluntary expression of women's sexuality in any other context, so the "lesbian" wife is not considered worthy of protection, and the "lesbian lover" appears to deserve "punishment."

Ignorance, harmful stereotyping, and homo-phobic labeling by the medical profession is another ongoing problem. One book on sexual abuse discussed the problematic case of a young woman "who ran off to become a lesbian after being sexually abused." This kind of prejudiced conclusion-drawing seriously hinders women survivors from coming out as lesbians and forces lesbians to deny their experiences of abuse. Calling lesbianism a "mental illness" also has a similar effect of obstructing the coming out process, and making it difficult for lesbians to seek counseling when in distress.

Another form of stereotyping, quite common in the straight feminist community, is to project the image of potential sexual abuser on lesbians who are "out." I have been called "degenerate" by women who hardly knew me, and I am not the only one. Some feminists hate the thought of lesbians participating in support groups or staying overnight in the same room at a women's conference out of fear that we might sexually objectify them. This type of homo-phobia, though unpleasant to say the least, can be overlooked as long as we have support, but it can be devastating to an isolated woman who is just coming out.

More subtle Freudian heterosexism can be just as harmful. I recently read a feminist article on "The Woman's Love Life-

Cycle" that categorized "homosexuality" as a teen-age phenomenon. Maybe it is true for some heterosexual women and men, but it surely cannot be universal!

Many groups that have professed to be sensitive to lesbian/gay issues still fail to reflect upon what they have learned in all other scopes of life, which is generally heterosexist. A typical example is a teachers' group involved in sex education that organized a series of seminars on diverse lifestyles. After taking up the subject of gay/lesbian students, they began to talk about how aging males needed sexual contact too, encouraging women to have a better understanding of the sexual needs of their partners.

Women's sexual health, sexual and emotional life, and quality of relationships are hardly ever mentioned in development issues, as if they were a limited luxury, valid only for the more industrially developed countries.

However much effort we make, there still is a considerable lack of awareness among both men and women regarding the fundamental rights of women and girls to determine whether or not, when, why, with whom and in what way they want to express their sexuality, or the women's right to enjoy sexual pleasure with respect for their emotional and physical integrity, regardless of socioeconomic status.

I hope I live to see the time when it becomes recognized that any violation of women's right to sexual self-determination is a grave human rights violation. This must include forcing or exerting strong social pressure on women to do such things as marry, bear children, undergo abortions, and have or not have sexual relations. All forms of legal, economical, social, religious and cultural discrimination that take place in the family, community, workplace and society against women who do not choose to conform, should be abolished or discouraged.

Lastly, any women's right to have a fulfilling sexual and emotional life, which may include love between women, should always be mentioned in women's health care considerations. Self-affirmation and support are the only effective measures against their problems.

13

The Past and Future of Unai, Sisters in Okinawa

Takazato Suzuyo

Women in Okinawa have a different identity from "Hondo women"—who live on the main islands of Japan—and this difference is deeply rooted in the history of Okinawa. Okinawa, which was formerly the Ryukyu Kingdom, has only recently been part of Japan. It was just 390 years ago that it was invaded by a clan from Satsuma, and some 120 years ago, in 1872, that it was formally annexed by Japan's Meiji government. Okinawa has managed to maintain a unique tradition and culture, which include performances and handicrafts that have been inherited over its history of cultural and commercial exchanges with China and other Asian countries.

The distance between women in Okinawa and those of the Hondo is rooted in their experiences and how they survived World War II and the postwar era. Okinawa experienced an appalling three-month ground battle at the closing of the war and, following defeat, was ruled for 27 years by the oppressive control of the U.S. military forces. On the Japanese mainland, after a shorter U.S. military occupation, a Peace Constitution and the Japan-U.S. Security Treaty were concluded. Okinawa was completely ignored in this decision-making process. Japan's rapid reconstruction from war devastation and economic growth was achieved at the cost of the victimization of Okinawa. In other words, Japan gained its prosperity by treating Okinawa as a scapegoat and turning it into "islands of the U.S. military bases."

Now, 23 years after the 1972 restoration to Japan, I would like to recapture the historical experiences of Okinawa from a woman's perspective and look at how Okinawan women are constructing our own identities. This should be accomplished by creating a rich global society through encountering and sharing with other women in Asia and other regions; by examining and exposing the nature of the military; and by organizing women's strengths and capabilities to create a world of nonviolence which will never require us to depend on military forces.

Structural Violence and Sexploitation by Military Forces

There are plans for a massive visit of 1,000 U.S. military veterans to Okinawa in June 1995. The veterans, who were in their 20s at the time of the war, will hold a commemoration ceremony at a U.S. base in Okinawa and will hoist the U.S. flag which they used when they landed on Okinawa. When this news was released, it caused tremendous consternation and anger among many Okinawan people. Above all, this forces women who were victims of an unimaginable violence to relive their pain. The United States, along with prime ministers from its former allies, such as France and the United Kingdom, held a large-scale memorial ceremony for the Normandy Landing Operation (D-Day) in June 1994, and following this were veterans' ceremonies and parades commemorating their victories in Guam, Saipan and the Philippines. What lies behind this series of activities is an ostentatious display of the armed forces of victors or liberators, and the reconfirmation of the political, economic and military leadership of the United States in the international community.

Okinawa underwent three dreadful months of ground battle when the U.S. military landed, resulting in the deaths of 200,000 people, including infants and elderly. Nonetheless, modern buildings have been constructed today, and the affluent daily life of the people has been restored. However, even now, daily activities on Okinawa are often disturbed by the excavation of large unexploded shells, about three hundred of which are found annually. Furthermore, it is estimated that the removal of remaining shells will take another fifty years. While Okinawa makes up only 0.6% of Japan's total land mass, 75% of active U.S. military facilities are concentrated in the area. People in Okinawa live under very tense circumstances, including the possibility of crashes by U.S. fighters, the constant roar of aircraft, the chance of forest fires or accidents caused by stray shots or shrapnel during drills with live bullets, as well as crimes by U.S. soldiers.

Among all the problems deriving from the U.S. military bases, the one which has been committed most continuously over the past 50 years in Okinawa involves sexual transgressions against women. Women survived bombardment during the war only to find themselves facing another kind of aggression. Soldiers trampled on women's bodies as they did on the island itself. There were numerous cases of rape. Some women were raped in the fields or on the sides of roads, or after being taken away from their families at gunpoint. Some were raped on the military bases where they were working as domestics or typists. Wherever the place and time, the sexual violence against women has resulted in pregnancies, murders, and mental disorders. How many of the veterans who plan to visit Okinawa will bear in mind the past crimes they committed against women? Even though they are now retired, 50 years ago were they not members of the military establishment that assaulted and raped women? The structural violence of the military forces is inseparable from their new actions, and we, the women of Okinawa, are making our refusal to allow their planned event very clear.

The suffering of Okinawan women, like that of the Koreans, Taiwanese, and Filipinas whom the Japanese government owes war compensation—the systematized sexual exploitation by military forces to encourage or reward soldiers' fighting spirit and as an outlet for their sexual desires—was covertly arranged and approved. Patriarchal or militarily oriented societies place women in a subordinate position and legitimate their objectification as sexual machinery in order to achieve the goals of the nation. The sexual victimization of women continues at military bases and in regions of conflict around the world today. The very nature of military forces, with their structural mechanisms of violence, should be fully uncovered so that the silencing of women can be ended and their pain healed.

What this means, first of all, is that it is necessary to dig up past crimes. The peace movement has demanded the removal of the bases, but in spite of the progress made it has neglected to recognize the gravity of the crimes and human rights violations against women. Hence the overwhelming majority of the victims have been unable to file cases, with the result that the statistical figures on these crimes fail to reflect the real situation, and in many cases offenders have been acquitted without contest. Taking into consideration the way in which the U.S. bases in Okinawa have functioned to provide sorties, communication, drilling, logistics and recreation for 50 years, during the Korean War, Vietnam War, Gulf War, and other regional conflicts in which the United States became involved, the significance of crimes by the military's 500,000 stationed soldiers and personnel has not been sufficiently understood, and has contributed to customs in Okinawa itself which undervalue women's human rights.

This year marks the 50th anniversary of the end of the war. Many newspapers have published special memorial issues with themes such as the experiences of survivors. However, even though crimes against women are social crimes, they have not become a theme and hence these publications have hushed up the past even today. This explains why the offenders, the military side, can march onto Okinawa with their banner a half century later. Currently women are determined to fill in this gap. Regardless of whether the crimes were committed during a state of war or during the postwar period on the military bases, the crimes must be investigated by the victims themselves.

Prostitution Sanctioned at the Bases

Women who had lost their husbands, elder brothers, or sons in the war, or who had been raped and lost their dignity, were driven into selling sex to American soldiers around the bases in Okinawa after the war. According to 1969 statistics, there were 7,400 such women. Considering the female population aged between 10 to 60, one in every 40 to 50 women was engaged in prostitution. Those women had no other choice other than to sell their bodies to the last drop of their blood, sweat and tears in order to feed their children and families, and to survive. Eventually, their hard work at the bottom supported the base-dependent economy of Okinawa, with no social consideration given to their contribution.

This society with military priorities allows people to be ruled by violence, weapons, and money. This includes the "Yumiko-chan Case" of 1955 in which a six-year-old girl was raped and murdered, as well as the numerous other rape victims and humiliated women. A woman who was raped by three American soldiers when she was 21 received plastic surgery several times in order to cover up "the stigma" and was repeatedly admitted to mental hospitals. She cried out: "I lost my humanity at the age of 21. But still I am a human. Please remember that." Another woman who engaged in prostitution for U.S. soldiers returning from Vietnam suffers from paranoia and has almost choked to death several times. She suffers from severe mental illness and stands in the rain and rubs her head on the ground saying, "I am an evil woman. I am too ashamed of myself. I am an obscene woman. Please, I am too ashamed of myself to face to others. I'm dirty. Please forgive me." She wandered around the streets day and night. We hear cries demanding restoration of deprived dignity. We would like to reveal the experience of Okinawan women following the bravery of Korean women who broke their 50 years of silence and began to tell their experiences of sexual slavery, which was long concealed by the Japanese Imperial Army.

War Crime Perspectives

In May 1993, a 19-year-old woman was taken into a base by car and raped. The case was reported only after the suspect who was arrested had fled to the United States. The bar association and the prefectural assembly took up the case. The alleged assailant was sent back from the United States, but the victim did not pursue the case. A military court in the United States in March 1994 gave the soldier a dishonorable discharge. According to police statistics, three to five rape cases are reported annually. These figures reveal only the tip of the iceberg, since for rape cases to be classified as a crime the victim must file a complaint for prosecution. Today, due to the economic reversal resulting from the yen's rise and the dollar's decline, young and poor American soldiers either approach women sexually with sham soft words or they resort to direct violence. They would find it hard to imagine how during the Vietnam War American soldiers were spending greenbacks like tissue and buying several women a night.

The soldiers stationed in Okinawa are not required to register as aliens so their period of stay in Japan is unknown. In the recent trend of "internationalization," many Japanese regard U.S. soldiers as friendly foreigners, and this is reinforced by images of movie heroes. Many local residents participate in carnivals and bazaars held on the bases. The number of applicants for colleges on the bases has increased, and young girls dream of the opportunity to court U.S. soldiers. Each soldier has a private room thanks to a special "consideration budget," which comes from the Japanese government's defense budget. Gate controls stopping young girls from entering bases have become looser. This policy of easing entrance to the bases seems just the opposite from the medical care measures taken to prevent American soldiers from getting venereal diseases when, taking advantage of the dollar's rise in value, they left bases to play around. However, it is in fact exactly the same in essence. The existence of the U.S. soldiers continues today, and the past violence of the soldiers has not been cured. It is a continuing nightmare.

As a result of changing economic relations between the U.S. military bases and Okinawa society resulting in reduced demand in areas surrounding the bases, the working conditions of working women, such as Filipinas with entertainment visas, have become harder and human rights violations have increased. Around 180 to 200 Filipinas with entertainment visas are working near Camp Hansen in Kin town, where two Filipinos died in a fire in 1983. Even though Okinawan women are (economically) equal to or superior in position to U.S. soldiers, they are still assaulted by groups of male soldiers directly or indirectly. Thus though the appearance has changed, the essential structure has not.

The World Human Rights Conference in Vienna in June 1993 gave recognition to the issues of "comfort women" and to the group rape of Muslim women by Serbian soldiers in Bosnia-Herzegovina as violations of women's human rights and labeled the women as victims of war crimes. I also made demands for effective measures. At the NGO Forum which was held simultaneously with the conference, various forms of violence against women were raised, requiring an expansion of the concept of human rights to include violence against women. This event encouraged a reinvestigation of the issue of violence against Okinawan women under the long period of control by the stationed U.S. military.

In regard to the rape of the 19-year-old girl, the Association for Solidarity with Asia called for an investigation based on the Vienna Declaration. In response, six women's organizations in Okinawa launched a joint petition campaign titled "The Statement to Investigate the Rape by a U.S. Soldier and a Demand for the Prevention of Crimes Against Women" and submitted this to the governor of Okinawa Prefecture in April 1994. In the statement Okinawan women demanded: (1) an investigation into the series of human rights violations against women by the military going back to the beginning, and efforts to help women put their lives back together, and (2) the initiation of counseling services for empowerment in order to restore the human dignity and ravaged bodies of women by both the Japanese and U.S. military.

A Warm Wind from Nairobi

The 1985 UN Conference on Women, which was held in Nairobi at the end of the UN Decade for Women, had a strong impact on the Okinawan women who joined the conference together with around 13,000 women from all over the world. Many women from various countries attended the workshop on prostitution and women's labor held by the "Okinawa Women's Association 1980." Women from around the world stood at the microphone and discussed their own problems and brought solidarity to all women at the workshop.

This warm wind in Nairobi again blew in Okinawa. The women's "Unai" (Sisterhood) Festival, initiated by a female radio director who is involved in the women's movement, was launched by networking individuals and grassroots woman's organizations over the radio. The group got financial support from local authorities and the women's festival was launched in 1985 under the joint sponsorship of a women's executive committee, a private radio station, and the city government. The festival aimed to create a new culture by and for women through the perspective of the Nairobi experience and grounded in Okinawan women's history. Now, in 1994, ten years has passed, and the Unai Festival will hold a workshop in Beijing at the Women's Conference in August.

The name *unai* derives from women's determination. Since time immemorial, sisters in families have been called *unai* and have been regarded as having great spiritual power. Thus, the birth of a daughter is considered precious. However, in this communal society that worships ancestors, there is the ceremonial responsibility of *totome* (a long wood card with ancestors' names in which the spirits reside), which stems from paternalistic kin relations in which the birth of the eldest son who will succeed the house is cherished. A woman who married the eldest son of the family was invariably expected to give birth to male children and had to continue giving birth until she bore a boy; if she failed to deliver, she would be divorced or would raise a male child conceived by her husband with another woman.

This deep-rooted custom of *totome* divided women into those who bore males and those who did not. Single women were buried in shabby graves on the roadside. Thus *totome* has been one basic source of indignity and deep sadness for women. On the other hand, rituals in communities were maintained by *noro* (female ritual moderators), and the spiritual power of women was highly regarded. Towels woven by women were respected as holy items that protected their husbands, brothers or lovers from danger while sailing or on a journey. It appears as if, at first glance, the men and women shared equal value, and the power between men and women was mutually supportive, but strictly speaking, the basis of this custom was the denial of femininity.

Okinawan women marked 1985 as "the first year of Unai" and declared that women will make and act upon their decisions in order to live their own lives and enable others to live. They took up the issues of peace, the environment, discrimination, customs, work and culture from women's viewpoints. On the day of the festival, about 60 to 80 organizations and groups gathered despite their different political beliefs and shared the same floor. Women's autonomy, independence, and networking are Unai's distinctive features. We said, "let's go out and play," and this became the principle of voluntary participation among those with similar intentions. The festival is like a tapestry of various groups and organizations, including labor activists, artists, feminists, and alternative natural childbirth groups, peace and human rights activists, a group for mother and children's issues, recycling groups, international cooperation groups, a women manager's society and a consumer cooperative. It is like a weaving that uses women's history as the weft and solidarity with women of Asia and the world as the weave. The festival is also a space for uncovering and expressing women's possibilities and capabilities for arts like one-woman plays, short plays, poster making, music, photography and movies; it is a space for interchange, for posing problems; it is action oriented, boldly challenging, and makes new findings.

Women's Spiritual Power on Radio

For the past ten years, a radio program titled "Twelve Hours of Radio by Women," made possible by the support and participation of private radio stations, has begun broadcasting theme music composed by women, who control the radio waves for 12 hours without interruption from 9 in the morning to 9 at night. From these 12 hours enormous possibilities develop. The program links many women and men, beyond space barriers, who otherwise could not participate in the festival due to their particular circumstances. Through the radio, participation of various people is made possible, including those who are at work; in hospitals; those taking care of children or patients; those in cars; or those in remote areas. Lectures, one-woman plays and concerts are on air simultaneously, and at symposiums, the participation of listeners is made possible through telephone lines. Ongoing workshops and participants' voices are spread all over the island simultaneously. Since Okinawa does not have electric trains or a subway, cars are used and people are connected to each other through the car radio. It is as if women's spiritual power on the radio waves has occupied Okinawa Island! The various types of programs that have been broadcast on this 12-hour radio program by women over the past ten years include: (1) one-minute speeches by 100 people, both women and men, on a different theme every year; (2) concerts by women singers from different genres; (3) Okinawan women's postwar history fashion shows with the radio as the stage; (4) a network of grass-roots women groups from other areas; (5) overseas telephone and radio telegram communications to Asian, and North and South American countries, (6) listening to the real voices of women working at marketplaces or on isolated islands.

What has emerged from the Unai Festival? Through the spirit of networking that was created, women have discovered their own powers and capabilities, and this has enabled them to realize that they can resolve various issues like peace and environmental problems and discrimination and to utilize each others' abilities.

The festival has also encouraged women to run for the local assembly and thus to act as major actors in solving problems. New businesses like weaving, dyeing, handicrafts, and recycling have been born, and linkages among groups with numerous associates among Asian peoples have been established. But what is most significant is that while support for the various activities grappled with and the coordination of various movements are developing slowly, they are definitely being connected.

Okinawa, a tiny island, is burdened with many problems and contradictions, but we hope to restore women's self-reliance and an island without army and military bases by revealing Okinawa to Asia and the rest of the world. It has been said for ages that the role of women in conducting rituals is *"Inaguya ikusa no sachibai"* (women lead to solve the battle). We will move toward a peaceful society from a perspective of women in which violence is denied with dignity and that reconciles human beings and nature. With this perspective, we shall work on immediate and concrete objectives.

14

Women and Alternatives to Agricultural Decline

Hikita Mitsuko

Shirataka, where I live, is a rural town in Tohoku, the northeastern region of Japan. At the center of the Okitama Basin, where the town lies, runs the Mogami, one of the longest rivers in the country. The area is surrounded by forested mountains and is rich in natural resources.

There are four distinct seasons. Summers are hot, and winters cold with heavy snow covering the ground for four months of the year. Local people have developed and maintained an agriculture and lifestyle based on these natural and geographical features.

Rice has long been a major crop. Mulberry trees and cocoons have been other major sources of employment. Until a few decades ago, weaving silk was a common side business for farming families. During this century, people began planting new crops, such as tobacco and hops; started raising livestock, including cattle, pigs and poultry; and growing fruits such as apples, pears and grapes. Until the 1970s, small-scale composite farming was common, with rice, the main crop, supplemented by some combination of these other crops.

For the last few decades, however, the area has seen remarkable change both in agriculture and in lifestyles. The government's industrialization and agricultural modernization policies have made agriculture a minor industry here as they have in most other agricultural areas in Japan. In the 1950s and 1960s, the chief male laborers in farming families became "*dekasegi,*"or migrant workers, during the winter season, engaging mostly in construction work in distant cities such as Tokyo, Yokohama and Nagoya. Eldest sons were generally expected to continue the family farm, but other farm children often chose nonagricultural occupations. Some moved to cities where they found employment with big companies. Others found jobs with nearby factories that manufactured electrical appliances or automobile parts or with other small-scale manufacturing businesses which were started as local agriculture declined.

Facing Agricultural Collapse

The government's liberalization policy, which intensified in the 1980s and 1990s, has driven agriculture closer to collapse. The number of farming families in my town has decreased to half of the total number of families.[1] People engaged in agriculture account for less than 20% of the total working population. Many full-time farmers have gone part-time, taking on sidelines in other industries. Most farming families have left the farming in the hands of elderly people. Young couples go out and earn money from jobs in local companies or public organizations, such as town offices and hospitals. They may help with farm work during the busy seasons.

As agriculture has gone from being a major to a minor industry, the traditional agricultural way of life is disappearing. In the past, the community was nearly self-sufficient in terms of food supply. Besides rice and vegetables grown at home, people picked wild plants and mushrooms in the nearby mountains. Food processing was another important domestic task. Beans were made into *miso* paste (soup stock) and *tofu* (bean curd). Seasonal vegetables were pickled. Large volumes of pickled and dried vegetables were stored away for winter. This lifestyle is disappearing as commercialism permeates the local community.

Even farming families now buy their food in supermarkets. Growing vegetables, picking wild plants, and pickling and drying vegetables have become pastimes rather than necessary domestic tasks and are usually done by elderly family members.

Working for a company means being away from the community, leaving little time for community labor such as mending irrigation facilities or weeding and pruning trees on common land. Community fire brigades, which are volunteer organizations consisting of local males in their 20s and 30s, now have difficulty recruiting and maintaining members due to the lack of a sense of community.

The processes of agricultural decline and lifestyle and community change are occurring at a rapid pace, but the traditional patriarchal form of farming families and people's consciousness remain basically unchanged. The position of women remains low both in the family and in the local community. Though women are involved in increasingly diverse occupations and they have some economic power, they are still treated as *yome*.[2] Most women are expected to live with their husband's family when they marry, and are expected to do housework and take care of children and older people in the household in addition to their own jobs. Their farming and domestic labor is not properly recognized, and they do not have a say in planning and management even when they are a major source of farm labor. When women engage in other occupations, their income is often considered to be part of the family income, which is administered by the head of the family (usually the husband's father or the husband). This person owns the farmland and property and at the same time manages the farming and home economy. When he dies, ownership of the land and the property usually is not passed on to his wife but to the first son.

Reluctant to be subsumed by the traditional patriarchal farming family, local single women have started to reject marriage to the successors of farming families. However, the idea that the first son must marry and continue the family farm is still strong, and some men, partly due to pressure from their family to continue the family line, marry women from other Asian countries such as the Philippines, Thailand, Korea and China whom they meet through the mediation of the town office or private marriage brokers. The number of such marriages is increasing. More than thirty men from my town have obtained brides via this system. There are over 700 foreign women married to Japanese living in Yamagata Prefecture. These marriages can now be seen in cities as well.

The power of Japan's yen may be part of what draws foreign women to rural areas. After marriage they encounter many of the same problems that local Japanese women do, and to these are added communication, language and cultural problems. There have been several cases in which, because of the hardships of being treated as *yome,* foreign women divorced their husbands and went back to their home countries or found jobs elsewhere in Japan and risked overstaying their visas.

The rural community is disintegrating. In its final struggle to maintain the remnant patriarchal family form, the rural community is outmatched by urbanization. Sooner or later, rural areas seem destined to become mere adjuncts to cities, functioning as residential and subindustrial areas with fewer family and community ties.

The Challenge for Women

Is there any chance that agriculture, rural life and community can be revived? To do so will require that people in rural areas alter the basic unit of the community—farming families. The patriarchal family will have to be replaced by a family based on equality and partnership between men and women and between generations. This process of change could foster individual creativity and initiative, especially that of women, and could revive agriculture, revitalize rural life and rebuild rural community.

A few efforts to seek an alternative are already being made locally. Women's initiatives in particular stand out. In my own town there is a group of farmers who about ten years ago started a sort of workers' collective to process their own agricultural products for sale during the winter. Their motive was to create an alternative to *dekasegi* work. Processing agricultural products not only gave them jobs during the winter, but also helped them to continue farming in other seasons because the members could buy agricultural products from each other at prices more favorable and stable than those of the market. Their main products are several kinds of local pickles and *mochi* (rice cake), which are sold mainly to consumers' cooperatives in a nearby city and in the Tokyo area. Their materials—rice and several kinds of vegetables—are produced by organic farming techniques, which use little or no agricultural chemicals.

More than half the members of the collective are women, and they have recruited more workers, mostly women. Some are older women who know how to make local pickles. The wages are above the local average. Pay is equal for men and women, new and old members. In the spring they negotiate with buyers (mostly consumers' cooperatives) on prices and volume of their processed products for the next year. Then they meet to decide what and how much to grow on their farms in order to provide for the group. The whole process is democratic, and newcomers, who are mostly women, learn to develop their own initiatives, an idea which was once rare in rural areas. The group helps individuals, both men and women, to develop their own agriculture and make a living.

Another recent local change is that some single women are choosing farming as an occupation. Some of the women are from farming families, but others are not from an agricultural background. (One Tokyo woman chose to be a farmer right after graduating from university.) In our town, where agriculture has been maintained through the inheritance system, this was traditionally unheard of. There have been cases, however, where single men or families without an agricultural background have started farming. This new development has shown a sign of women's initiatives in agriculture and indicated possibilities for new ways of rural life, based on the freedom of individuals rather than on the ties of a patriarchal family.

However, at present there are still many obstacles for would be farmers who do not come from agricultural backgrounds. This is especially true of obtaining farmland, due to the inheritance system. Acquiring various kinds of farm tools and machinery is also costly. For local agriculture to be revived, various forms of support are needed, not only from individuals but from local governments as well. Newcomers need help in accessing farmland and farming equipment more easily and cheaply and in learning agricultural techniques effectively.

Women hold the key to the future. The future of agricultural life depends on how much independence and freedom women can gain and enjoy and the initiatives they take toward creating alternative agriculture and rural community. In the past, women were used as labor to develop agriculture and maintain an agricultural life, but in the future they must be the creators of a new agriculture and rural life.

Notes

1. According to the agricultural census, a farming family is a household engaged in farming, with a total farming area of more than 10 acres, which earns an annual income amounting to ¥100,000 or more. It includes families where only one or a few family members are engaged in farming.

2. The Japanese character for *yome* pictures a woman inside a family. Women in Japan, when married, are more often regarded as women belonging to their husbands' families than as independent women.

III

Voices of Women

15

Commitments to Women's and Buraku Issues

Suzuki Mieko

The International Movement Against All Forms of Discrimination and Racism (IMADR) was established in January 1988 at the initiative of the Buraku Liberation League (BLL), a group which struggles to protect the rights and improve the situation of the burakumin, a caste in Japan whose members have long been victims of discriminatory treatment. Since I was a member of the BLL, I became involved in IMADR during its formative stages. At the time I was working at a company, but was very interested in finding a job working for an international organization dealing with minority and discrimination issues.

Currently, IMADR is trying to promote the exchange of information between indigenous and minority groups, analyzing and researching the common aspects of the issues concerning these groups and then formulating concrete steps to be taken. In the course of this work, we hope to create an overall network of groups suffering from discrimination. IMADR's main concern is not in taking new action but rather in linking existing movements of groups that have been victims of discrimination. For example, we have linked Asian indigenous people and Japanese groups as well as Japanese and American minority groups. When we say Japanese minority groups, we refer to the burakumin, the Ainu, permanent foreign residents (mostly from Korea) and migrant workers.

The problems of discrimination and minority groups are often difficult to solve within the boundaries of a single nation-state. South Africa is probably the clearest example of this, since domestic policies changed because of pressure from the international community. Consequently, international solidarity is extremely important. By coming into contact with other groups dealing with discrimination in other parts of the world, I have come to realize the value of solidarity with these groups and have felt their relative weakness within their own countries.

From the outside, BLL activities are probably viewed as male-dominated, and I don't think that BLL is unique among Japanese social activist groups in this respect. However, it is very clear that in reality, these movements are supported by women at the grassroots, community level. Yet at the decision-making level, few women participate. At both the local and national levels, the situation is the same. Women play a supporting role, but it is rare for them to take on visible leadership. Consequently, the present male-dominated society is reflected in these social movements, influencing their organizational structure, style of activism, and concerns.

To address these concerns, the BLL has allotted special seats for women on the central steering committee at the national level. However, the number of these seats still only number 2 out of 18. At the local and prefectural levels, we only have one female chairperson. Women are able to attain the number two position but are hardly able to reach the top.

Another problem is that there is a prevalent belief among BLL members that women's issues should be discussed among members of a women's department, which consists entirely of women. Consequently, many BLL members still believe that the women's issues are something that only women should deal with. This kind of thinking also prevents women from joining high-level decision-making bodies.

I think it is a huge problem that although women have a central role in BLL, they are not able to influence its overall structure. This is common in many social activist groups. Community-based movements, in particular, are supported by women. Consequently, it is necessary for more women to actively participate in the decision-making process, which could be encouraged through the implementation of a quota system. At the same time, unless the organization takes the initiative to remove the obstacles which prevent women's participation, the situation will not change. For example, our community meetings are held at night, but it is very difficult for women to attend them. In particular, women in their thirties who work as well as hold domestic responsibilities, taking care of children and the household, cannot participate. Consequently, an important question is how the organization can solve these kinds of problems and encourage women's participation.

The BLL is primarily an organization fighting against buraku discrimination, but other kinds of discrimination also come into play. Among these, discrimination against women is a major concern. However, it is difficult even for us women to know how to deal with this issue. Activists in the women's movement always encourage those of us who are fighting for the rights of buraku, Ainu or Korean-Japanese to fight more for the rights of women within these larger movements. I understand their position, but we cannot see giving priority to one form of discrimination over another. We feel that we are discriminated against as women as well as in our position as burakumin. It is not an issue of which problem is greater. Consequently, I react adversely to the suggestion that we should be acting more on behalf of women within the buraku movement. I agree that women's issues have not been dealt with adequately, but I also feel that it is wrong to try to separate the two issues and make us choose which is more important. This problem is very difficult, but it is definitely something which we must deal with.

With regard to women's issues, many problems can be raised, such as participation in the labor market and sexual harassment. However, the way in which one deals with these issues depends on the perspective from which one views them or the reality surrounding oneself. For example, in dealing with women's labor, for many women the issue of sexual harassment may be the most important concern in the workplace. However, for buraku women, finding and securing work is still the crucial issue. Consequently, I think it is important that women raise many different issues, based on their various interpretations of the situation, but few realize this. People in the women's movement need to try to understand the mutual relationship between the women's struggle and the buraku movement within the overall context of Japanese social discrimination.

I think that Japanese feminists have a limited perspective. Since the movement lacks breadth at the grassroots level, their experience and understanding are also limited. The economic and social background of these "middle-class feminists," and, consequently, their perspectives, are also very different from those of the buraku women. Recognizing these differences is crucial. I think that feminists in Japan are lacking in terms of their understanding of minority issues and the structure of discrimination. That is why many of them are reluctant to get involved in the *Tennosei* (imperial system) issue. It is clear that women should not be afraid of voicing their different perspectives on these issues.

16

Looking at Sexual Slavery from a *Zainichi* Perspective

Kim Pu Ja

I am a member of the Yosong Net, or more formally the Uli-Yosong (Korean Women) Network on Comfort Women, which was founded in November 1991. All the members are Korean residents in Japan (or *zainichi*), though we also have Japanese supporters. Our goal is to study and resolve the issue of "comfort women," or forced military prostitutes during World War II, by reexamining racism and sexism from our zainichi perspective. In 1990, Yun Chong Ok, from the Korean Council on the Matter of Comfort Women, came to Japan, and we were so impressed by her speech that we founded our Yosong Net.

Our aims for 1995, the 50th anniversary of the end of World War II, are as follows: to get the Japanese government to take responsibility for compensating the former "comfort women" and, more generally, to abolish sexism and racism. The Japanese government should give official compensation because what happened was a national crime. We will continue to fight for this cause as long as former "comfort women" remain alive.

Various women have been attracted to our group—activists and nonactivists alike, people with citizenship in the Democratic People's Republic of Korea (North Korea) and the Republic of Korea (South Korea). Of course, this is partially because there is an eagerness to solve the problem, but I think it also results from the fact that there is no place now for all *zainichi* women to gather. In the past, the zainichi community has been divided into two organizations—the Group of Korean Residents in Japan (Mindan), which is aligned with South Korea, and the General Association of Korean Residents in Japan (Soren), which is close to North Korea. *Zainichi* women were bound by this framework as well, but in the 1980s, the grassroots women's movement influenced us to reconsider our positions and overcome this structure. In a feminist spirit, we began to consider the "comfort women" as something that we should take up. We decided that the North and South Koreas were fictional and that women from both sides of the divide needed to join hands to fight together. We consider this issue crucial for our past, present and future, especially in dealing with the issues of sexism and racism.

Individuals have the right to make decisions on how they want to conduct their own lives and sexuality. The Japanese government violated these rights when it victimized the "comfort women." It is clear that these women had no choice in how they would conduct their lives and sexuality. Many Korean girls were deceived during the colonial period. If we should gain anything from this experience, it should be to learn that people have the right to decide these things for themselves.

Until now, *zainichi* people have failed to go beyond simply criticizing Japanese society, but we now realize the necessity of criticizing sexism within our own community as well. Many *zainichi* men believe that the "comfort women" issue is solely a racial one, but this is not the case. Why, for instance, did the former "comfort women" remain silent for half a century? Why did these women in North and South Korea remain hidden? It is largely because of patriarchal Korean society. Prostitution exists in our own male-dominated society. The same can be said for the *zainichi* community itself, and we need to be critical of our own society.

In the beginning, these ideas were rejected out of hand by *zainichi* people, but Korean men need to be held accountable for sexism as much as their Japanese counterparts. Being a victim of discrimination does not give a person carte blanche for discriminating against others. This consciousness is vital for the building of an anti-discrimination movement. Coming into contact with gay and disabled people has helped me to realize how my own ignorance was at the root of my biases. It is clear to me that ignorance is the cause of discrimination. I think that this is the basis upon which we *zainichi* women are participating in the "comfort women" movement.

Zainichi society is changing, and is becoming more diverse. With the 1984 amendment of the Nationality Law, our community has come to encompass people of a variety of nationalities— some South Koreans, some North Koreans and more recently some Koreans who hold Japanese nationality. There are at present quite a few *zainichi* people working as public servants, including some in the Ministry of Foreign Affairs. Many with North or South Korean citizenship try to conceal their backgrounds, whereas some with Japanese nationality do not even use their native Korean names. We can thus see that there are various ways of expressing our identity, and I think this is a good sign.

Our greatest concern now is the education of the next generation. Concretely speaking, we would like our children to be assured of receiving an ethnic education. We believe this should be a right for people attending Japanese public schools. Japanese schools now support the Japanese government, and only "normal" Japanese children can attend them. Korean and disabled children are excluded. We have to change this and make schools serve the needs of all residents. I believe that schools should be for all residents, regardless of nationality or disability.

My sense that Japanese schools serve Japanese citizens alone was confirmed last spring when my son received a "school announcement" (Japanese children receive something called a "school notification" while for *zainichi* children it is called an "announcement") addressed to his Japanese-style name. I interpreted this as meaning that they expected us to register him in school under this name. I complained about this, and the officials promised that they would revise these regulations. I believe, fundamentally, that things are this way because schools are for the benefit of Japanese citizens and the Japanese government.

I also believe that ethnic identity should be an important part of education, not just for *zainichi* children but for the majority Japanese, who need to be taught the reality of history. Consequently, we believe that the issue of World War II compensation is important for reeducating Japanese. In other words, the "comfort women" can be a key to uncovering the victimization which occurred during the Pacific War.

We will not be able to change things if we cannot radically change the way Japanese view the war. Until there is a change in the idea that the Japanese were victims of the war and that they liberated the Asian colonies, war compensation will be impossible, both spiritually and monetarily. If these things change, then compensation may become possible.

From a *zainichi* perspective, the Japanese invasion into Asia did not begin with the fifteen-year war (which began in 1931 with the invasion of Manchuria and ended with the surrender in 1945) but rather started with the Sino-Japanese War (1894) and the Russo-Japanese War (1904). The Japanese need to reexamine their history and take these facts into consideration. After the Sino- and the Russo-Japanese wars, Japan made Taiwan and Korea into colonies, and then invaded China in order to establish the Greater East Asia Co-prosperity Sphere. Consequently, unless Japanese begin to see these two wars as the beginning of colonization, they will not be able to understand the significance of war compensation to Koreans and Taiwanese, nor even why *zainichi* are in Japan.

17

My Work as an Ainu Woman

Keira Tomoko

My work is that of Ainu women—all of the small tasks of daily life. I weave mats, embroider, cook, prepare for the *kamuynomi* (prayer for the gods), etc. In earlier times, the *kamuynomi*, hunting, and fishing were men's work. Women were not allowed to perform these tasks. Of course, when there were no men, older women performed the ceremony in their place.

Throughout Ainu culture, there has traditionally been a division of labor between men and women. Men and women worked together, adhering to these traditional roles. I believe these distinctions are not a form of discrimination. At first I was uncomfortable with these ideas, but as I became more familiar with Ainu culture, I realized that it is through the combination of the spheres of women and men that the overall Ainu world is formed. Consequently, I am no longer resistant. I don't think that women are looked down on because only men are allowed to perform the *kamuynomi*. When it is performed the first god to whom respects are paid is Ape Huchi Kamuy, a female god of fire. Ainu also believe that home (*chise*) is the domain of women and that the woman is the overseer (*chisekor katkemat*). Consequently, men are just residents of the house and are obliged by female overseers to pray.

As Ainu try to reclaim their traditional culture, the first step is to try to restore the original order of Ainu society. Only later does it become possible to try to reevaluate and revise the traditional roles of this society. In order to restore the rights of Ainu women, we need to decide what the conditions are for being an Ainu woman. We cannot say we are Ainu women unless we have our own mountains where we can gather our wood and grass. Cooking foods purchased at supermarkets is the role of modern women, not of traditional Ainu women.

In Ainu culture, women are prohibited from brewing wine and from participating in the *kamuynomi* while they are menstruating. This is not because woman is impure. The idea that "women are impure" comes from Buddhist teaching and is not an Ainu idea. I think it is true for indigenous people's culture throughout the world to clearly distinguish the tasks that a woman can and cannot do during menstruation. One reason for this is to lighten the burden on women's bodies during this period. A woman who has gone through menopause is called *huchi;* these women are able to pray at the *kamuynomi* and are given respect. Women who have passed their period of sexuality are treated as if they are closer to the gods. That is why I think the Ainu regard menstruation as important.

I believe that reviving the spirit of *kamuynomi* in our daily life is what is most important, not just speaking the Ainu language. Being able to speak Ainu or perform the *kamuynomi* is meaningless if there is no sense of humanity for fellow humans. Consequently, I believe that priority should be given to understanding and internalizing this rather than to learning the Ainu language.

We do not simply want to revive Ainu life as it was. Since the majority of Ainu marry Japanese, if Ainu culture is simply handed down to Ainu, it will probably vanish. We hope that children who are raised as Ainu as well as children who are not but who are aware of Ainu culture can grow up together, mutually understanding each other in this society. Our organization, Yay Yukar Park, is trying to create a space where this will be possible. We hope that the numbers of Japanese who understand Ainu crafts and culture will increase and that this will be handed down to Ainu children of future.

18

Mizura: Providing Service to Women in Yokohama

Abe Hiroko

Mizura, a space for women, has two objectives: to provide counseling services to women and to provide space for groups to use for free. Our counseling service policy is to listen to what the clients have to say without imposing our values on them and to support them in making their own decisions, as well as to stay in contact with the client until the problem is solved. In some cases, this might just involve offering suggestions over the phone for fifteen minutes or so. Settling or solving other cases requires us to take concrete action. For example, in dealing with claims from women suddenly and unfairly dismissed from work, the tactic used is to suggest the claimant join a women's union affiliated with us. This suggestion is made because women can join the union individually but bargain collectively. In the case of women fleeing from violent husbands, we provide shelter for the women and their children, if any. Once they are safe, we start consultations.

The problems facing women foreign nationals are becoming more diverse, yet the first thing that most women need is still a place to flee. This is one of the reasons we maintain a space. After finding out what the woman wants to do, we can provide assistance. For instance, if a woman wants to return to her country, we help her get her passport back, find resources for travel expenses, and contact NGOs back in her home country to follow through on her case. In the beginning, we handled cases of human smuggling and forced prostitution of Thai women. However, as international marriages have increased, we have been facing more and more with problems between husbands and wives. We also help handle various processes surrounding matters of residence, such as obtaining visas, or establishing the nationality of children. In short, we respond to concrete and immediate needs.

Mizura's members are women who work and live in Kanagawa Prefecture. Provided with the tools necessary for us to achieve our goals, such as an office, office equipment, and a permanent staff, we can do a variety of things. This is a space where members can freely initiate and conduct new projects. We have meetings related to office administration, but the staff does not direct the members' activities. They take responsibility for their own activities. For example, when some members want to have regular study group meetings on certain topics, they can use the space to inform and contact others. Study groups are held on sexual harassment, women's bodies and Eastern medicine, and energy issues, such as nuclear power plants. Members conduct their projects, such as group counseling, freely and creatively. While consultation services are our main activity, our space is available for members' activities.

The establishment of Mizura's office developed out of the activities surrounding the issue of amendments to the Labor Standards Law in the early 1980s. At that time there were two active groups: "the Kanagawa Association Against the Equal Employment Opportunity Law" and the "Japanese Women's Caucus Against War, Kanagawa," who were holding study sessions and meetings, attending Diet meetings, and lobbying Diet members. After the Equal Employment Opportunity Law took effect, we were having a hard time finding new perspectives on how to protect the rights of individual working women and how to improve those rights. Labor unions were not taking up women's issues to any significant degree. Given this situation, we decided to have a gathering of concerned people who wanted to explore possible paths. That was in 1988. For the following year, we thought out what we wanted to do and how we could confront the problems that women face. We were not sure whether we would succeed or not, but we decided to try.

There was no precedent in the nongovernmental sector on which to model our response to these issues. But we felt there was a need, and, more than that, we wanted to do this by and for ourselves. We wanted to work together to solve problems that women face. We wanted to try to find solutions through trial and error and through our own efforts. We also wanted to meet other women and learn from them. Those feelings were strong in us. We created Mizura in 1990 with the desire for it to be a place where people's promises and secrets would be respected, where no one would be imposed upon, and where we would go when we were in trouble.

Once Mizura was under way we started receiving an unbelievable number of requests for help. We did not know our own ability until we tried. Though women are beginning to receive some recognition in society and in the workplace, we are still thought of as incompetent. Men have definite responsibilities and make decisions in many areas. However, I think that even very capable women are distanced from the opportunity or the experience of being in charge and of seeing a project through. But once we tried, we realized that we could do it. Women's capabilities are brought out by cooperation. We are more competent than we thought or realized. In carefully responding to our cases, we became more aware of certain civil rights which would be of use to us in our future work. At the start, we set up the office using money gathered only from individual membership fees. Creating a paid staff was a dream. Some said even if it is a dream, it's a dream we can achieve. At our general assembly one year later, the tone of our voices had changed, and we were more confident and assured. We started with eighty members, and now after five years, there are approximately five hundred members.

The core members who set up the office were all active in the student movement in the late 1960s and were committed to women's issues. They were workers who were able to stay on the job without being squeezed out when they reached the age where they were expected to marry and have children. We had all been involved in various movements. I myself was active in the student movement and local struggles, and it was in this environment that I encountered *"ribu,"* or Women's Lib. I took a breath of the movement's fresh air but it wasn't to my taste.

I think the women's movement before the 1960s was, roughly speaking, a movement aimed at institutionalizing policies and women's rights. What the Women's Lib movement proposed was for women to become subjects. It seemed that in one sense, it was for women a first step toward establishing their status as women or as individuals. It opened their eyes to their own inherent worth, not in terms of comparison to men. This thinking influenced many people who were committed to social change and to liberation movements. The Women's Lib movement gave birth to many new ideas. But when asked if you participated in the Lib movement, you wondered what it really was. Back then there was a wide variety of activities taking place on university campuses and in other places. People got together for training and other gatherings and formed groups. We cannot say exactly what a true liberation movement was. But the influence of the idea of fostering women's individuality and self-acceptance was very strong.

Later, during the 1980s, when more and more women began joining the workforce, other problems began cropping up. By now, women have recovered and seem to be heading in the direction of making decisions by themselves, while gaining community with other women. During the 1980s and 1990s imported feminist theories were rampant. Many women were interested in these theories and read and debated about them. Then they faced the question of how to put theory into practice.

The impact of International Women's Year (IWY) was certainly immense. It triggered an international effort that culminated in the Convention on the Elimination of All Forms of

Discrimination Against Women. There were people who created a national plan of action and participated in the IWY Conference. Some women deal with amending laws, some protested against discrimination against women in the media and; some are active in unions or citizens' movements; and others like us, are involved in helping women solve their problems as individuals through small-scale counseling activities. The women's movement has really became diversified.

In a sense, we at Mizura consider ourselves as part of the human rights service sector. NGOs are a new sphere of the service sector. They must greatly increase in number so that our existence can be recognized socially. Ideally there should be so many NGOs that help is always just around the corner and so that people have a choice whether they want services from the government or from citizens' groups that deal with human rights problems. We hope that the number of NGOs increases to the point where NGOs and similar organizations compete to improve quality, and cooperate with the government while maintaining a certain distance. On the other hand, we would like NGOs to maintain their openness so that people not previously involved in NGO work can participate in them. People should have a choice of organizations to turn to or to participate in. I think this can become key to creating participatory local governments.

19

Promoting Women's Participation in Yokohama

Sakurai Yoko

There are approximately 600 organizations in Japan which are associated with women's activities. Of these, 200 are associated with the Ministry of Labor and are known as "houses for working women"; another 200 with the Ministry of Agriculture, Forestry and Fisheries and are called "houses for farming women"; and the remaining 200 are called "women's centers." Generally speaking, these women's centers are run by prefectural or city governments. Only one, the National Women's Education Center, is a national institution.

Progress in women's activities and the establishment of relevant associations can be divided into three different stages. The first began right after the end of World War II, and can be characterized as a period of local women community members building private institutions. These grassroots private institutions soon encountered financial difficulties and tried to raise additional funds by running side business, such as managing parking garages or reception halls, but they failed to achieve effective results.

The second stage emerged in the 1970s in response to the International Year and UN Decade for Women. Local governments started to realize the importance of constructing a functional hub for women's activities and began building women's centers to fulfill this role.

The current stage can be described as the boom of "women's centers." The women's centers institutionalized during this stage are publicly financed, but their actual management is carried out by private groups. Forum Yokohama is one of the products of this third stage; it is 100% financed by the City of Yokohama and led by a women's association in Yokohama. The Yokohama Women's Association for Communication and Networking (YWACN) is supported by taxes collected from Yokohama residents, but since our association is not a city-owned institution, members are recruited not by public workers but by our own full-time employees. This can be seen as a step up from the second stage.

The role of women's centers seems to have changed along with these three phases. During the second stage, the UN Decade for Women, the movement emphasized the importance of women's involvement in social activities, but the real consequence was only participation in educational functions. Women attended lectures in order to promote their social consciousness, but did not seem to be able to go beyond these study workshops. The main objective of women's centers was never intended to be simply a hub for educational activities for women; it was meant to provide them with opportunities for engaging in political and labor activities. This was also supposed to create support and understanding among men. During the second stage, these ideas were not successfully incorporated into their definitions of women's roles, and this seems to be the reason why autonomous committees were not able to establish independent associations.

This does not mean, though, that the women's centers in the third stage are fully aware of their objectives. They are still unclear as to what their true tasks should be within their communities, and this is why many members of women's centers from all over Japan come to visit Forum Yokohama. We try to increase the consciousness among women that their participation in society is important. We have courses called "seeing the light at the end of the tunnel," meaning that we try to help people relate their past experiences to finding solutions to our current problems.

We need to have our courses lead women to financial independence and social progress. This is the main goal of Forum Yokohama.

The actual activities of the Women's Association in Yokohama are planned by our own staff members in their own respective departments. Most of our staff members were recruited through public notices. Generally speaking, in Japan, it is difficult for women who want to commit themselves to women's activities to be able to explore their ambitions, unless they become professors and give lectures. We try to provide women with an opportunity to fulfill their motivations. One of the qualifications to become a staff member is age. Applicants must not be over 50 years old, since we would like them to be committed to our work for at least 10 years. The myth that younger people are necessary is hard to break.

Although our financial source is Yokohama City, we do not just follow the requests of those who are there but try to pursue our own interests and concerns. Since our staff members have professional knowledge and broad networks, the city has been very cooperative and has made efforts to reach a mutual consensus. We have made efforts to establish this sort of relation by introducing the self-evaluation standard. We are fully aware that our functions are financed by taxes, and try to do our best given our capacity. Our staff members are assigned to submit an annual report, which becomes the fundamental scheme for the following year. In recognition of our planning efforts, Yokohama City has often accepted proposals and has been very cooperative.

The Women's Association in Yokohama was established as a third sector organization under the umbrella of the local administration. The main reason for this is that labor costs are lower in the third sector than for official city staff. Another reason is the ability to utilize private human resources. Our ties with the administration are sometimes criticized, but given the situation in Japan, they are inevitable if we are to secure employees and a stable income to support our activities. Organizations like ours, which can get financial support or subsidies, have no choice but to work as core centers for other independent organizations. Since we rely on financial support from the local government, one of our concerns is to support NGOs that are trying to remain financially independent.

The Women's Center has been described as an institution which encourages women's social participation. There is no common understanding, however, on the level at which the Center should work. I don't think giving seminars and lectures for women is enough. I believe that it should function as a think tank and propose policies concerning women. Regarding women's participation in politics, it is still very difficult for us to voice our opinions at the national and prefectural level, and we still do not have the opportunity or place to create collective ideas about policy-making. Whether the Women's Center will be a place for women's collective force is not a question to be discussed here. But I myself believe that the Women's Center should develop a solid scheme to create a community not only for women members but also for men. This fundamental program should lead the Women's Center to a leading role in our community.

20

Photography from a Woman's Perspective

Ooishi Yoshino

When I first began working as a photographer, I noticed that there was a general belief that female photographers were inferior to their male counterparts. This feeling still exists, of course, but it was much worse at that time. It was thought that men were supposed to take pictures and that women were supposed to have their pictures taken. Why, then, would any woman bother to take pictures? That's really the way it was.

There were some people who encouraged me to persevere, but not many. It is thanks to them that I am doing what I do today.

The status of women, not just in photography but in society as a whole, improved somewhat during the UN Decade for Woman. There were substantial differences between the situation women faced prior to the Decade and the situation that developed afterward. In the earlier period there were movements such as Chupiren (a women's group in early 1970s, demanding the right to abortion and free access to the pill) in which women could express themselves, and I guess that these Women's Lib movements provided the basis for what would come later. The Japanese social system itself increasingly began to recognize the rights of women. This development has been obvious in the past five or six years. Large newspaper conglomerates are now hiring women. I feel that society as a whole has begun to change.

I went to Vietnam in 1966, at the height of the war. I felt somehow that I needed to meet and photograph the people there. I feel strongly that political violence and war are horrible problems, but I wanted to portray the faces of life in the midst of tragedy. Some people photograph beautiful and famous people, but I feel that it is those who are overlooked who make history. I aim my lens at voiceless people [*Voiceless People* is the name of Ooishi's collection of photographs taken in Cambodia.—Ed.] because these very ordinary people bear great burdens, and I want those who see my pictures to appreciate this. I photograph ordinary life at times of conflict, but this does not mean that I am saying war is not frightening. Those who live in such difficult situations learn to go beyond the fear and live in spite of it. They bear deep wounds, but learn to overcome them. This admirable human capacity is half of what I want to convey. I also want to say that although these people are smiling on the outside, war and political violence create deep wounds in people, so these problems must therefore be a concern for all of us. Because of the wounds, people smile on the outside, but in their hearts they find it difficult to laugh. This is the other half of what I want to convey.

I am often asked about what it means to have a women's perspective, but having been a woman all my life, I find it difficult to know in what way it is different from a man's perspective. I believe that there are men who have the same perspective on things as I do, and I also think that gender aside, perspectives vary from individual to individual. Roughly speaking, though, women live life close to the bone. In the case of photography, for instance, women can just take pictures, but because men live in a somewhat detached way from the root of life, even their photography tends to become a theoretical matter. One can perhaps say that men live mostly in their own heads. This is because of the way they are brought up, but it is a big difference. When people say "a women's perspective," I interpret it as meaning perhaps that when women write or take photographs, they do not overlook the little details of everyday life.

Yet when I get caught up in big issues that involve politics or economics, I feel weak. I wonder if this is because I'm a woman. Of course, politics is a creation of people, and for that reason, I have great interest, but politics is overwhelmingly a burden for those ordinary people I spoke of earlier. Their lives are stable and then become unstable. It is for this reason alone that economics and politics exist, and in this sense I am interested in politics and economics. I have often visited other countries in Asia, and of course my interest in Japanese economics and politics stems from the fact that the economic and political situation in Japan has an influence on all of Asia. Having been born and brought up in Japan, I am very concerned about this country; at the same time, I think that Japan can have a large effect on the rest of Asia. Japanese people as a whole are becoming egotists. Our intention to protect ourselves is paradoxically expressed as egotism. This fact has a great bearing on the rest of Asia, and it is something that I am deeply concerned about.

And from now on? I will continue to do the things I have always done. I guess the countries and localities will change, but the theme will remain the same. For some time to come, I would like to convey the thoughts, feelings and lives of people. Of course, doing so is emotionally tiring, and there are times when it becomes too heavy and serious a burden. However, once I do it, I feel that I have to do it again. As long as I have the physical strength, therefore, it is what I will continue to do.

21

A Cooperative Restaurant
on the Miura Coast

Ishiwatari Sadako

I think it is quite unique, even on a national scale, for a women's group from a fishermen's cooperative association to run a restaurant. The idea to open a restaurant within the Miura Fishermen's Cooperative Association was conceived during the Sagami Bay Urban Resort Festival in 1990 while we were discussing the survival of fishermen, given increasing imports triggered by trade liberalization. We decided to try to create a more urban-style fishing industry by starting some new businesses in the port, and we opened a small seafood restaurant as an experiment.

We began holding cooking classes to promote the consumption of fish before opening the restaurant and worked to explain the high nutritional value of fish and to emphasize the importance of eating fish from our own neighboring sea. The city of Miura then suggested that we begin using the restaurant as a place not just to teach cooking but to learn how to turn fish dishes into commercial products and to test their value. We opened a restaurant two months later, with the support of the municipal government. Thirty members from the Women's Group took turns running the restaurant.

We eventually earned a reputation as a restaurant with a warm atmosphere in which people could enjoy homemade dishes made by fishermen's wives. We gained the confidence of our community. My own desire for the Women's Group to open a restaurant independently of the government grew stronger after the success of this trial.

Later, the city government gave our Women's Group charge of managing a Citizens' Information Center. Half a year later, we negotiated with the municipal government and obtained permission to use part of the Information Center building for a restaurant, and it opened in April 1992. Eleven members from the Women's Group now take turns working there. The hourly wage is ¥660, though it increases on holidays and for overtime work. We have never been in the red.

The fishing industry is in trouble all over the country. Everybody is working hard to survive, and Miura is no exception. Many people who have been in the industry since they were young have had to stop fishing involuntarily because of government policies to reduce the number of fishing ships. I think that men have been encouraged by the women who continue to work and survive in the midst of such severe conditions. When the Women's Group started its campaign to promote fish consumption 15 years ago, what motivated us was the hope of stopping the general trend toward not eating fish and to alleviate the need to make increasingly big catches because of the falling price of fish. We thought we needed to develop some fish dishes that could go well with bread. Our movement got on track about ten years ago. Now we hold cooking classes every month.

Another activity of the Women's Group has been fighting environmental pollution in the sea. We want to win back the beauty of the ocean. We have been campaigning against synthetic detergent since the 1980s and are now trying to promote the recycling of used cooking oil in collaboration with our local government. We collect used oil from houses and take it to a soap factory, where it is recycled into soap powder. Eight women's organizations in the city have joined us in this movement.

We recycle clothes as well. We collect old clothes and give them to traders. Some clothes are reused for materials, and some are exported to Southeast Asia. This campaign was started by a women's organization called the Society for the Betterment of Life. As a member of the city council, I then proposed that the local administration and citizens' groups work together in these efforts. In 1994 the collaboration started. Clothes are collected in each district three times a year when the residents bring them to designated places.

The Women's Group is thus engaged in a wide range of activities at the core of citizens' organizations. Miura City used to have few sewage system installations, and when I became a member of the city council I began advocating the importance of a sewage system for the protection of the ocean. Because I was the first and only female member of the city council, which has 24 members, I think I can present a different viewpoint from the municipal government. I said that if we continued polluting the ocean, we would lose our inshore fishery. I said that we needed to give due consideration to fish breeding grounds along the coast, since they would never recover should we let them be ruined. I showed the council some photographs of the shoreline covered with detergent bubbles. Once the dirty water annihilates laver, wakame-seaweed, and shellfish, it will be too late. Laver, once a popular food in this area, has become a luxury item because the catch has decreased. It is not the same shore we used to have.

The Miura Fishermen's Cooperative Association is thinking of expanding its fishing into a compound industry. Otherwise young people will not be attracted to the industry. There's an enterprising spirit in the association now. That's why I hope our restaurant will be an important foothold for revitalizing the industry, utilizing this wonderful location.

Fishermen's cooperative associations have mostly male members, because the law requires that members fish at least 90 days a year. This requirement, however, will soon be altered. So far, two women have become leaders of associations. I think there will be female chairpersons in the near future.

The Women's Group was originally formed in response to our

consensus on the need to start saving up for hard times. We set up a credit association, which has spread all over the country. Now the Women's Group and Miura Association are working together and selling "Wakashio-soap." We have grown and awakened to the importance of protecting the ocean from pollution. Because of this awareness, the role we play is important.

The women's subgroups of fishermen's associations in the different regions have their own characteristics. There is a big difference, for instance, between offshore fishery and coastal fishery, which uses only small boats. Members of some fishermen's associations even have vessels for leisure fishing. In the case of small boats, some leave in the morning and return in the evening of the same day. Most women working at our restaurant are the wives of fishermen engaged in offshore fishery who had to stop fishing because of the government policies to reduce catches. Those women hope to stay connected to the sea in some way.

There are 900 members in the Women's Group today. Many of them cannot join our activities because of their regional differences. I think it is important for us to concentrate on what we can do in each area, and do it well. It would be great if every beach had a fishermen's restaurant like ours.

22

A Women's Space in Sapporo

Kondo Keiko and Makishita Noriko

The Women's Space opened on May 1, 1993. We had been preparing for the opening for about six months, but it was really the culmination of the twenty years of work and continuous experiences in the women's movement in the area around Sapporo. This movement began in the late 1960s, when the Women's Lib movement was coming of age. In the intervening years, women who were active in those movements have built up their own strong internal networks, but each group has had its own problems to deal with. The more they became involved in understanding and investigating those problems, the more difficult they found it to solve the problems alone. For the last ten years, therefore, there has been a shared desire to create a stronger, wider support network.

At the moment we have 180 members, most in their thirties, forties, and fifties. All the members have their own backgrounds in the activities they have chosen to focus on, and some have jobs in local administrative bodies. The members also have their own networks, which help them to provide information or know-how to solve problems brought up for consultations or requests to the Space. The purpose of our work here is to organize this information and networks.

In addition, we conduct negotiations with various local public administrations. In August 1994, we organized a local women's labor union and have started collective bargaining with companies in the area. We have tried to direct our movement in such a way as to fully use the capabilities and expertise of our members to help solve situations in which the problems confronted by women have slipped through the cracks of the system.

Experience has taught us how difficult it is to overcome the barriers set up by the local government. While carrying out activities in support of foreign women, we have found a necessity for daily consultation and shelter services; the same is true for people fleeing from sexual violence. In the past, the best we could do was to cooperate based on our individual connections. We found, therefore, the need to create a "space" in the form of a socially active movement.

Makishita: My work as an arbitrator at Family Court exposed me to shocks daily as I became aware of the terrible conditions faced by women. The women who came to Family Court were all housewives, but they were always in hard-to-understand situations, so Family Court simply could not solve their problems. A typical issue that came up was the question of what kind of life divorced women face. I felt that we needed to bring these problems faced by women to light as social issues, and started thinking that we needed some kind of organization to coordinate our movement.

After World War II, women gained various social rights, yet housewives were excluded. It is true that with the passage of time, those women have begun to question the fairness of the situation they are supposed to endure. The reasons leading to divorce, however, have not changed a bit: love affairs, domestic violence and gambling debts incurred by husbands.

Of course, there is one change at least: nowadays women have begun to file for divorce instead of just putting up with their situations, but the point is that the causes that lead to their divorces remain the same. This is what we need to change, and in order to address and help solve those problems we need a movement like ours.

Kondo: One of the main focuses of the Women's Space is consultation, and we divide it into two main categories. The first covers sexual violence (rape, family violence, for instance), and the other covers labor problems particular to women (unfair dismissals, sexual harassment, etc.). Our concrete activities include accepting people in need of help, supporting their efforts to start a new life, helping them to negotiate with the local government, and supporting their struggles if their cases go to court.

Our second area of activity is supporting the efforts of various women's groups who meet at our office. For example, we support the activities of groups doing feminist counseling, projects against child prostitution, projects to help school dropouts, and projects to help women participate in politics.

The third area of our work includes our own social investigations and organizing our meetings.

Makishita: The local government offers its own consultation services at women's centers, for instance, and in some cases recommends that the women go to psychiatrists. This is often ineffective, however, and they come to us for advice. In some cases, while they are talking with us here, they suddenly realize why the psychiatrists could not help them—it is because doctors, as well as people in administrative offices, look at things from a man's point of view, and their way of settling the problem reflects that mindset. This is why women feel unsatisfied. In contrast, our organization looks at things completely from the viewpoint of women.

Kondo: In this male-oriented society, the viewpoint of men has even been internalized into women. "Women of understanding" are precisely those who are assigned to administration office windows. They are the people who give advice to housewives, telling them to be a little bit more patient.

Those who come to see us have already endured too much. They come for advice because their patience is already exhausted. Why would they need to come here if their situation were bearable? This is how they feel.

At present, therefore, we are demanding that feminist counselors be assigned to the windows of the administrative offices. We are also planning to train feminist counselors; people with the ability to see and judge a situation completely from the viewpoint of women and who can understand women's feelings.

Makishita: Speaking concretely, when women go to a police station to seek refuge and protection against their husband's violence, they are told the police don't handle quarrels between spouses. This happens all the time. Here, at the Women's Space we don't handle such matters that way, and we don't tell women to be patient, that's for sure!

Kondo: Nowadays, as far as human rights are concerned, the school and the home are extraterritorial places, or black boxes. Coincidentally, most of the people suffering in these places are female students and women. This may sound incredible, but we know of many cases of sexual violence committed by fathers or stepfathers that the police have refused to deal with as crimes.

Makishita: The other day we went to the Labor Standards Inspection Office to talk about a case where a company refused to pay wages to its foreign laborers. As a result of our negotiations, the office opened a counter to deal with labor problems and consultations for foreigners, and it is now open twice a week. Despite the fact that it only deals in English, I think we've achieved a great success.

Kondo: We intend to get feminist counselors assigned at least at the Women's Center in Sapporo City and at the Women's Activity Center which is run by the Hokkaido Administration.

We would also like to see counselors at the Mental Health Center, where the "be patient" policy prevails.

Makishita: Cases are sometimes referred to us by those centers or by the police. In rape cases, where the statute of limitations has expired, for example, the police send victims to us, telling them they might be able to take civil action, but that they are powerless beyond that.

People working at the Women's Center in Sapporo City also come here to talk with us. The city administration advocates the idea that gender equality is a fundamental need in our society. Unfortunately, their way of trying to achieve it is very superficial; it is only trends in society that make them feel they should make full use of the abilities of women. In addition, their initiative has been carried out under the leadership of men. What we would like to do is pursue women's activities without the restrictions of municipal policy, but by making full use of their organization and facilities. Their policy is still nothing more than a mood, but we will make progress by utilizing each other's capabilities.

Kondo: Men often talk about "co-existence between men and women," but this is not a subject to be taken lightly. The situation in Hokkaido does not even go as far as this, since there is no policy for women. There is still a "Juvenile and Women Section," meaning they still maintain the concept of "Women and Children." But considering the fact that the administration there has started to ask us to provide lecturers, we will continue to state our opinions clearly to the public, making the most of whatever we can use.

From now on, our main purpose will be to establish a strong network between women in Southeast Asia and women in Hokkaido, and with that purpose in mind we will be attending the coming UN Conference on Women in Beijing.

In regard to carrying our movement forward in Japan, we have invited people from Korea and the Philippines whenever we have found that we were confronting common problems. What is needed in the future, however, is for us to go there ourselves and make the necessary connections to work together to continue advancing our movements.

We need to create long-lasting cooperation and common policies to deal with various problems, such as children of mixed blood, especially Japanese-Filipino children, forced prostitution during the war, and children's prostitution. We would like to see the Women's Conference in Beijing become the starting point for achieving these goals.

23

Apron: A Restaurant Run by Women

Taguchi Atsuko

It was in 1982, 13 years ago, that we opened the restaurant and lunch catering shop called "Apron" in Zama City. Twenty-three women and one man are working there today. The sole man, who is mentally disabled, was referred to us by the city's Welfare Service Department. In the case of Apron, however, it would be more appropriate to say that 24 people are sharing the work rather than that 24 people are doing 24 individual jobs.

The founders got the idea of starting the shop from a course on women's independence that was being offered at an autonomous school called Zaso Academy (Zama and Sagamihara). They wanted to do something in order to achieve economic independence. They first opened a store called Green Peace where they served a fixed menu and sold small crafts made by women. More than a dozen people provided the funds to open the shop. I was not one of the founding members, but joined the venture later. Green Peace was eventually dissolved and grew into a variety of independent projects: one member, for instance, is conducting a yoga class.

I decided that it would be nice to have a restaurant in my own community where people could have safe meals, so a friend of mine and I rented a small space, just 30 square meters or so, and began to offer a fixed menu. We didn't even have the funds to remodel the place, which was previously a "snack bar," and we used tableware donated by friends.

To be very honest, I am not a very good cook. At the beginning, we had few customers, and people were whispering that we would soon go under. They said that we had started the venture recklessly, without any prior experience. Gradually, however, our restaurant grew into a place where local people could get to know each other and become friends, and before we knew it, we were busy day and night. After three years we were able to manage with an hourly wage of ¥450.

I had some working experience, but had quit my job when I got married, as this seemed the natural thing to do. My husband's parents had both worked, so he was actually surprised at my decision. "Are you really going to quit?" he had asked me. He was very moved, however, to see me putting all my energy into housework preparing meals for him and polishing his shoes. Then, one day, I suddenly told him I wanted to go back to work. Thereafter, we began to have quarrels every day. He changed, however, and has since become the kind of person who does lots of things, such as planting a kitchen garden and sharing fresh vegetables with our neighbors. He once said, "They are really shining," when he saw the women working at Apron, and it seemed that something had changed in him.

In 1987, the landlord forced Apron to move out, and we found our present location. Five women invested, and we began a "*bento*" (lunch box) delivery service. Our reputation spread by word of mouth, and soon city offices, welfare institutions and companies in our community were ordering our lunches. As the shop space doubled, the sales also doubled. We now take long vacations during the New Year holiday, for instance, but our customers are loyal. I think it is because we have gained their trust since our food is safe, healthy and tasty.

Five years after Apron moved to the new place, one of the founding members decided to open a new shop, saying, "I have become bored with Apron, as it is a success." She now runs a place which we consider a sister shop. I hope to see more and more shops like hers, where elderly people and men who live away from their families on job assignments can have safe and good meals, and where women can find a place to work.

The women from Apron met through our children's junior high school PTA. There were several divisions at the PTA, and I was in charge of the Adult Committee, which plans and organizes seminars. Violence in the schools was a big issue at that time. There was even an instance at a place close to us where a principal sued a group of pupils. We developed close relationships with each other as we talked frankly about our own troubles and our worries over issues such as bullying, sickness, and school and family troubles. We found that we had many worries in common. By talking seriously and candidly, we found that we could share these experiences and thus help to solve the problems. When one person confided that her child had been shoplifting, others suggested that she try to understand what had made him do it rather than simply criticizing him. One person's child failed an entrance examination, and the others encouraged her, saying, "It doesn't matter so much, does it?" In this way we encouraged each other and learned what was important.

With the exception of the one mentally disabled man, the 23 persons working at Apron are all women in their 30s, 40s, and 50s. All are part-timers, and we earn an hourly wage of ¥900, or ¥1,000 for early morning and night hours. The owners, meaning the investors, however, have the final decision-making responsibility, and thus get a small extra benefit. In this sense we are not totally equal. In spite of the fact that Apron is a place where each member carries a responsibility, rather than simply being a cog in a machine, there are some people who find this responsibility a burden. We don't find the same expectations and commitment to Apron among all the women. We found we needed to clarify who was responsible for doing tiresome work. It was a process of trial and error on our part to create a form of management which would not impose "commitment" on others or burden others with our own expectations.

We have a meeting once a month. Our principle is that anybody can say whatever he or she wants to say. At times this makes it seem like we are quarreling, and it is true that not all the members can put their thoughts forward in a straightforward manner. There are some people who find it hard to participate in discussions. In addition, there are differences among members in personality, experience, habits, and expectations toward Apron. Some have a deeper involvement than others in their work. It may seem easy to express one's opinion, but in fact it can be difficult.

The older people tend to have more energy. I sometimes wonder whether this has to do with the fact that they experienced the immediate postwar period, when they had to procure everything by themselves. As for the younger people, the more isolated they are, the more difficult it is for them to open their minds up. At recent PTA meetings, I have found that there is an atmosphere where those who speak out find themselves alienated. Parents seem to be divided as individuals.

We have recently come to feel that the Japanese tax system acts as a drag on women, and in particular, denies housewives the opportunity to work. Most of the members' husbands are salaried men, and "dependent family members" are exempted from income tax as long as they do not earn more than ¥1 million annually. If they earn more than this their income becomes taxable. In the case of Apron, this means that the members find it very difficult to work any more than four or five hours, five days a week. Women are forced to choose between being tax-exempt dependents, and independent people with a taxable income. I find that this discourages women from working. Even women who wish to become independent find it difficult to cross this threshold. I think that anybody choosing not to be a dependent family members will find it necessary to earn ¥1.5 million, but it isn't until you have an income of about ¥2 million that you can really feel independent. This tax system keeps the wages of part-timers from rising. Housewives remain housewives and are used as low-wage part-timers. In this way migrant workers and housewife part-timers have been tactfully?

Apron has prospered up until now, but I think we now have to consider how we can each work according our own physical strength, and how we can work together as good colleagues, accepting each other's way of working. We need to do this even if our sales stagnate or even decrease.

I was hospitalized once when I dislocated a hip. The other women I met in the hospital all told me they had lost their jobs. I really felt at that moment that the only reason I was able to continue my work was because we had created our jobs ourselves. Some people say to me, "You are merely earning money" or "Why don't you do some volunteer work, since your business has gotten on track." I think our most important achievement, however, is that women have created their own work place, which become a place where they can meet good people and build good relationships.

24

Working at a Consumer Cooperative

Arimura Junko

I was born during the baby boom. Social movements were quite active during my youth, so I always had much interest in them. I am interested in making a commitment to Japanese society, and have been thinking about how to create an alternative way of living. I decided to live a different life from that of other women. I decided not to have any children and not to work in a big company. I was born and grew up in a company town, and I knew the hardships of life under the network of companies and of being tied into community and kin relationships. This is why I chose not to become an employee of a big company. Another idea I had was to break with the ordinary relationship between men and women. I have been living with my husband for a long time. We have repeated divorces and marriages at our convenience. We registered our marriage when we needed, for example, to get a job, which means we use the koseki (family registration) system at our own will.

In the 1970s I encountered the feminist movement, which stressed women's sexuality and emphasized that women could give birth. I decided to have children and become a housewife.

I got involved in the activities of Seikatsu Club because I was looking for safe food for my small children. At that time, problems resulting from consuming polluted food, such as the

Minamata disease and those related to food additives, began to be exposed. We took a big risk by raising children in this society. Our environment is far from satisfactory in terms of raising children.

The mainstream consumer movement was initiated just by mothers. I was attracted to the Seikatsu Club because it seemed to aim at changing society. It was very interesting to read its magazines because they discussed the situation of Japanese society and what to do, and they were talking about society from all viewpoints, not just those of wives or women. Most of the consumer movements that target housewives provide only simple explanations of their activities because they think housewives can neither understand difficult things nor have enough time to read. But the Seikatsu Club does not discriminate against housewives in this way. And the Seikatsu Club uses the term of "*seikatsusha*" (living person) instead of "consumer." I felt that I could agree with these ideas.

I was happy to understand that collective buying is a starting point for changing society and that this is what the Seikatsu Club is about. Until then I had never known any movement in which I could get involved without giving up my private life. I was impressed by the Seikatsu Club because we could change society by making collective purchase and at the same time raise our children better. In short, I found that I would be able to create an alternative life by controlling our own food production, not just through consumption. We can realize this by purchasing eggs, milk, meat and so on that are produced in accordance with our beliefs.

Our way of purchasing food is very different from buying food from supermarkets. We have to order the food one month beforehand, and have to go get it at the place the ordered food is provided. This way of buying food in a capitalist society is nearly unimaginable. However, this leads the way toward creating an alternative society based on a new relation between consumption and production through the initiatives of "*seikatsusha*," or citizens. Rearing healthy children and living a healthy life will lead to changes in society; this is the ideology of the Seikatsu Club.

It is hard to find control or autonomy to this extent outside the Seikatsu Club. We get used to selling our time as wage laborers and buying and eating food as consumers. But now we can choose the producers of our food and have the food made the way we want. We started an autonomous life by creating things, not just by choosing them. This is our experiment in an alternative life and economy.

In our activities, we mainly do collective purchasing of food. But eating food is only one part of our life. We challenge all aspects of life in order to change society. We are also involved in politics through the issues of waste and detergents. I think politics should be a citizen's way of carrying out demands. But the problems related to our lives have never been discussed in politics. We questioned this and started our movement.

Some of our other activities include collectives in which we are trying to find an alternative way of working. The question of work is a life-long issue. We are trying to socialize the "shadow work," or domestic work. Of course, I do not think that all domestic work should be done by women. But at this moment, most of it is being done by women. So we started doing services to help domestic labor. We hope these services will lead to the creation of participatory welfare in the coming aging society. We are trying to create workers' collectives for domestic labor and to present our way of working as a model for society and to build up communities in the cities where we can help each other.

The Seikastu Club has about 50,000 members in Kanagawa Prefecture, and most of them are women. We divide our members into small units. Each unit has about a thousand members. And each member shares the responsibility for running the unit. Because the members pay a membership fee, they are the owners of the unit. They have the rights and obligations in terms of what each unit is doing.

All members participate in the management of the club. It was quite important for me, as someone who had always been no more than a wage laborer in our corporate society, which is dominated by men, to participate in management.

We can get involved in activities with our children, and these activities enable us to control our own lives. We can actually feel that we ourselves are the main actors in our lives. I think that women can fully excise their creativity and abilities at the Seikatsu Club. This point is most important among all the activities of the Seikatsu Club. All the members, are at the same time, investors. So without members' participation, there is no one else who has the right or obligation to run the club. There are no specialists on how to run a cooperative among the members. The members' participation is the only actor which runs the club. I think there are only a few participatory organizations run by women who actually decide and act.

I do not deny the negative aspects of being a housewife. But we are really concerned with children and food. So you cannot easily say whether being a housewife is good or not. It is no wonder that the Seikatsu Club, which operates as a cooperative for people who are worrying about their daily lives, places a priority on people's lives.

The Seikatsu Club does not affirm the division of labor between women and men in the present society, so we help women do domestic work at first, but we want to change the division of labor. And we want to change this corporate society. There are great possibilities for the Seikatsu Club as one group working for the creation of an alternative society.

25

Fighting Back Against Serving Tea

Fukuma Yuko

I work for Kawasaki City, in the health insurance section, and I am also the secretary general of the women's section of our trade union. It seems clear to me that there is a tendency for men to monopolize the "tasty" jobs. For instance, men draw up the budgets, whereas women, who are considered assistants, are placed in charge of general affairs.

At the Kawasaki City office, there are few women in managerial positions. Of the 22 people working in my section, 14 are men and eight are women. Only one of the managers is female, and even she was only placed there because the city government wanted to do something about the scarcity of women in such positions.

Another issue we face is something we dubbed the *Ochakumi* problem. *Ochakumi* means serving tea to guests or to our colleagues. At our workplace, *Ochakumi* is only done by women. In other words, female workers are regarded simply as tea-ladies. In my office, the female staff have to serve tea to all their colleagues and wash all the tea cups three times a day—at 8:30 and 10:00 in the morning and at 3:00 in the afternoon. *Ochakumi* was not a stated duty, but we felt it as a semi-obligation. When women applied for positions, they were asked what they thought about *Ochakumi* (naturally, men would not be asked such a question). If a woman said she would refuse to participate in *Ochakumi*, there was a chance she would not be hir_ !. If she replied that she would, this became sort of a declaration of intent. In any case, she would feel considerable pressure.

Until three or four years ago, almost all the sections had an *Ochakumi* system. When a female staff member was assigned to her section, the first thing she was taught how to do was *Ochakumi*, including catering to the tastes of the section members. But I think young women didn't like doing it.

In 1991, I brought up the *Ochakumi* problem at our trade union meeting. All the participants, I discovered, were very interested in this problem. So we—I along with my friends—prepared a questionnaire about it in order to discover the feelings of female workers, analyzed their answers, and presented our analysis in the union newsletter.

As a result, the system was abolished in some branches, and in others they changed the system, either by taking turns or by reducing the number of *Ochakumi* from four a day to just one.

I think, however, that the problem is deeper and more structural, and involves the sexual division of labor. We may be able to solve the *Ochakumi* problem but this larger structure still exists. This structure is our next target.

When I was a student, I worked in the peace and ecology movements, and then became aware of feminism and the Women's Lib movement.

I believe that feminism means thoughts and practices that liberate women. I have a high opinion about the Women's Lib movement in the 1970s. In a sense, I was saved by it. Others involved in it had respect for themselves, and thought by themselves. That is very important. The spirit of Women's Lib should be passed on from generation to generation.

26

From Child-Care to Local Politics

Tomizawa Yoshiko

I had a child in 1983. After my maternity leave was over, I decided to enroll my baby in a day nursery, but none of the public facilities in Suginami Ward, Tokyo, would take an eight-week-old child. The only places I could find were private nurseries, where the conditions were poor, so I found myself in a tight spot. I had to choose whether or not to resign from my job. Until that time I had believed the nursery care system was an elementary issue in the equality between men and women and had thought it was more advanced. The social conditions that would allow women with children to continue to work simply did not exist.

I and some other women went to negotiate with the ward mayor, but an official there said, on the record, "It is natural for mothers to take care of their children until they have reached the age of three. We pity babies who are sent to day nurseries right after the end of maternity leave. There is no need to build day nurseries for eight-week-old babies." I was very surprised at the low level of understanding this officer had of women's issues, especially since we had had the International Women's Year and the government was being urged to ratify the Convention for Elimination of All Forms of Discrimination Against Woman.

This jolted me into the realization that there was a wide gap between our movement and the actual conditions in our community. Women's liberation had not filtered in. In nursery schools, children were being taught that boys had to behave like men and girls like women. The viewpoint of sexual equality did not seem to exist in day nursery education or in the study of children. I thought that perhaps this was the reason that women's liberation has not moved forward in our country. As a result, we began to approach subjects familiar to us.

Many feminists I know decided not to have children as a result of the Women's Lib movement. As a result, I have found that many women who do have children are prejudiced against the idea of women's liberation. It is a sort of taboo and has not spread among them at all.

I therefore came to believe that women needed to participate in politics. In 1989 I helped a friend who was running in the Metropolitan Assembly election. I was very happy to have been able to help make a feminist a member of the assembly. I came to believe that we could change realities if women would become assembly members.

In line with this thinking, I accepted the urgings of my friends and ran in the ward council elections with the endorsement of the Social Democratic Party of Japan (SDPJ). I thought the SDPJ would understand me easily because its policy on women's issues seemed to be similar to mine. When I joined the party, however, I found that they could not understand me at all. For instance, one of the policies of the party was the elimination of discrimination against illegitimate children, but when I said that I wanted to take up this issue in the assembly, another SDPJ councilman said, "It's stupid to discuss such a trivial issue. Get out of here!" Part-time labor among women is a major issue for the party, but when I tried to argue against the planned lay-off of 900 part-time workers who had been on the job for three years, they stopped me from speaking. When I tried to ask a question about the rights of foreign residents, they told me to stop, that I had a "radical" opinion. The other members of the council had ties with the administration and had no interest in digging up new issues. At this time, I had been a SDPJ member for slightly over a year. They told me, "You are the only one who advocates sexual equality."

In addition, the members of the Democratic Socialist Party (DSP) always hooted at me when I spoke. Finally, a member of the SDPJ said, "We have tried to coordinate our efforts with the DSP, but they hoot at everything you say. We won't let you speak anymore." They robbed me of the right to speak.

In Suginami Ward, there were 52 council members, but only eight were women. I was the only one who took up sexual discrimination as a major issue. One day a female member of the SDPJ said to me, "Sexual equality has been achieved." The other female members involved themselves in issues such as school lunches, the environment, and the construction of streets and facilities in the neighborhood, and like male members, spoke as representatives of shopowners, landowners, and consumers (housewives). It was not until I became a member that I realized that the local council was so conservative that it represented only the conservative class. They presented no arguments against the long-term plans of the administration.

Suginami Ward is a commuter district. There are many working wives in the district, but they are so busy that they have no time to let the local administration hear their voices. The policy on women is geared toward housewives because these middle class women have a greater opportunity to take part in local politics. There was no women's hall, but there were consumer centers and civic centers that could be used in the daytime. The local people, therefore, had no way to understand how difficult it was for women to continue to work and that the rights of working women were not upheld because of sexual inequality. Working women's voices were not heard in the local council.

After becoming a councilwoman, I tried to get the local government to protect working women so that women could continue to work and tried to get them to think about how we could change gender roles. As a result, the officials in charge of policies toward women created materials and moved to make a women's action plan. A promotion center for sexual equality is now in the planning stage.

I am now considering the problem of how this center will be used. I have visited some women's centers in other areas, and I hope it will not be used as a cultural center for women, but instead as a center for lecture classes promoting changes in women's consciousness. I have continued to hammer the staff with this message, and things have begun to change, albeit slowly.

What I am calling for is the construction of a social environment in which women can continue to work and of a society where a variety of lifestyles, including those of foreigners and of dropouts, are respected. In Japan both men and women work so hard that it is easier for women to be housewives and rear their children. Women who continue to work must be in very good health or have mothers who can take care of their children. Therefore, the destruction of the value system which says that men work and women do the housework and take care of the children still makes it very difficult for women to choose a way of living from among many choices. Most members of the council, however, believed that paternalism is natural, so these issues were not discussed.

We are now organizing a network of local councilwomen called "The League of Feminist Members of the Council." Women on the council who share common problems can use this to communicate with each other and to respond quickly to calls. Just recently we issued a complaint to the minister of health and welfare and the director general of the social insurance agency concerning a pamphlet it published. The pamphlet, with a circulation of 1,800,000, is issued every year to recruit new adults into the National Pension Plan. The pamphlet read, "Women quit their jobs after they get married, so they become insured under the third plan and are supported by their husbands' pensions." I posed a question about this issue in the council and others did the same in their own local councils. We said that it was strange that the pamphlet pushed the idea that woman should give up their jobs after getting married and, in addition, complained that the drawing of the women, which was smaller than that of the man, was an instance of sexual discrimination. We succeeded in improving the pamphlet.

I have also informed other members in various areas about the problem of discrimination against the children of unmarried parents. In Japan there is a system of residence registers, and children are listed on their parents' cards. Up until recently, children of married couples were listed as "first son," "first daughter," "second son," and so on, whereas children who were born out of wedlock were listed simply as "child." This became a mark of shame which was used against them in school and in jobs, for instance. I told the members of our network to ask questions concerning family relationship as listed in residence registers because this is a topic of interest for local governments. From what I heard, in many cases this was the first time that this issue was brought up at the councils. One member reported that the mayor was surprised, saying he had never heard of such discrimination. As a result of these efforts, the system was changed so that starting this year all children will be listed as "child." The discrimination remains in the Family Registration Act, but the change on the residence card is very important since this is the document that typically must be produced when a person wants to get a job or get married.

In this case, the fact that citizen's movements and the councils worked in close cooperation brought good results. Of course, we appealed our case not only to the local councils but to the National Diet as well. I think we will be able to bring gradual change to our society if the number of members who sympathize with us increases and if we can continue to cooperate. I think women have come to take a place in the worlds of media, law, and politics, precisely because of the accusations they have brought against the discrimination which has always caused them to be overlooked.

Index